Federal Central Banks

A Comparison of the US Federal Reserve and the European Central Bank

A Report of the Banking and Monetary Committee of the Global Policy Institute written and compiled by Andrew Black, Michael Lloyd, Viara Bojkova and Sam Whimster

((forumpress

© Forum Press 2018

Forum Press is the imprint of the Global Policy Institute, London.
www.gpilondon.com

ISBN: 978-1-9071441-0-3

A catalogue record for this book is available from the British Library.

Design by Ben Eldridge www.bitmap.co.uk

Printed by Lightning Source www.lightningsource.com

Contents

Federal Central Banks

Preface

This report was funded jointly by the James Madison Charitable Trust and the Federal Trust for Education and Research.
In the light of the educational remit of these two bodies we
have tried, as best as possible, to make this report readable and
understandable by the non-expert. Federal systems are something of a specialist topic in political science and the language
of central bankers has risen to new heights of complexity and,
for many, mystification. Taking the two subjects together,
paradoxically, allows for some simplification. Both political
federalism and central banking are caught in a dynamic
between centralizing tendencies and the requirement to meet
the needs of all citizens across large territorial units. Our aim
has been to lay this dynamic open to public inspection.

The research was carried out throughout 2017. It uses predominantly secondary sources. Time and resources have not allowed for the generation of new empirical data or the modelling of counterfactual scenarios. There is a lot more that could be said, and there are important research topics that need to be developed further. There has been a coalescence between central banker discourse and political orthodoxy which we think has not be healthy for citizen democracy. This is an area that requires open-minded research and debate, and more of it.

The research team is varied in age, background, experience and disciplines – also in viewpoints. In arguing these differences through, we hope to have produced something more comprehensible than the usual well-worked specialism. We are particularly grateful to Terry Bishop at the Madison Charitable Trust and Brendan Donnelly at the Federal Trust for their financial support and their patience in allowing us to find our way through this challenging subject.

Sam Whimster
February 2018
Emeritus Professor, Gobal Policy Institute

Main Points

- The Report investigates the role of central banks in federal and confederal political systems, specifically a comparison of the European Central Bank with the US Federal Reserve.
- Federal and confederal political systems have a dual obligation, both to operate as an effective state system and to be responsive to the economic and political demands of their regional parts.
- Central banks, when considered historically, show problems of design and implementation, and adjustment to economic crises as well as capture by prevalent economic doctrines and interests.
- Central banks were given their independence in Europe

with the introduction of the Euro and the ECB. This followed the lead of the Bundesbank.

- Transferring the Bundesbank model to the Eurozone ignored its embedding in Germany's successful federal political system. Monetary and fiscal policies followed technocratic rules unchecked by democratic accountability.
- The US Federal Reserve achieved operational independence in the early 1950s. However, when faced with crises, the Fed has frequently been overridden by politicians and the Treasury.
- The Global Financial Crisis is no exception to this. Other measures, not under the instigation of the Fed, were required to 'save' the situation. It would be incorrect to argue that the Fed alone managed to 'save the system' from itself.
- The Eurozone, when faced with the same crisis, performed worse than the USA, and both areas used extraordinary measures to save parts of the system to the detriment of citizens' economic welfare and security.
- Unconventional monetary policy has been twinned with the imposition of austerity measures, in Europe the reinforcement of the Fiscal Compact. This has retarded recovery and exacerbated disparities in the Eurozone.
- Central bank policies have had perverse effects on property prices, migration and geographical mobility.
- The ECB did what it took to stop the EZ from breaking up. Greece and the periphery countries were saved but at considerable political and human cost.
- The crisis threw up constitutional and operational issues for the ECB made more difficult by the confederal structure of the EU.
- Steps taken to resolve the GFC have, in the main, strengthened federalist trends within the EZ and EU

economy. But these still have to be worked through at the confederal level where different interpretations of confederalism are in conflict.

- In particular, the lack of a EU Minister of Finance and Treasury materially slowed down the rate at which the crisis was resolved – or could be resolved in any future crisis.
- Democratic accountability should offset the increasing power of federal institutions and make monetary policies more accountable to citizens.

Executive Summary

Central banks have been with us historically for a few centuries, for as long as sovereign governments (initially kings) required funding for wars. With the growth and centralization of the modern state, central banks correspondingly grew to meet the borrowing and expenditure needs of government as well as taking on the role of regulating and meeting the credit and currency needs of national economies. The international aspect of central banks has undergone major switches from allegiance to the gold standard to the rules and disciplines of the Bretton Woods system. In the latter, central banks in the advanced economies were subject to Treasury and parliamentary control as part of citizen democracies. In the most recent phase starting in the

1990s central banks have become, ostensibly, independent of government, with a key role in controlling inflation, managing economic growth, sustaining the increasingly complex financial system, and influencing the value of the currency. The task of managing aggregate demand appears to have been handed over to central banks. In particular this raises questions of an institutional and democratic nature for confederal and federal systems of governance.

In this study we have examined two key central banks, the Federal Reserve in the US and the European Central Bank in the Eurozone, specifically chosen to illustrate their inter-relation with a federal and, respectively, confederal political system. There is a mutual interrelation between the degree of political federalism and the coordinating features of central bank. In addition, in the long history of continental-size political systems there is considerable fluctuation in the degree of centrality acceptable to the citizen base. In the light of this comparative platform we provide an analysis of the operational effectiveness of each central bank in relation to the financial sector and the real economy, with particular attention to the aftermath of the global financial crisis.

The picture that emerges is one of a confusing techno-cratic and financial operational nexus, not least in central bankers' use of an esoteric language which is used to justify and explain the role of central banks prior to, and after, the global financial crisis. In the US though there is a stable, if unwieldy, federal structure and a nominally democratic accountability to Congress, nonetheless the increasing tech-nocratic autonomy of the Federal Reserve gives cause for concern. The runaway development of the financial sector, formal and informal, over recent decades, has both chal-lenged the Federal Reserve and has also led to the accretion of its power.

One of the questions we have tackled in the study has been whether this accretion of power has undercut effective democratic control. Another question has been how effective has been the control of the financial sector by the Federal Reserve. And, thirdly, the extent to which monetary policy alone is capable of managing aggregate demand without the integrated support of fiscal policy. This is particularly the case in federal systems, and even more so in confederal systems, where the relative autonomy of the states making up the federation/confederation and the need to protect the economic and social welfare of their citizens is a political and democratic concern.

In answering all three questions in relation to the role of the Fed, we have been critical of the lack of democratic political control; the still overweening power of the financial sector, perhaps exacerbated by the use of quantitative easing, including the latter's uncertain impact on macro-regional development and wealth inequality, and the inadequacy of monetary policy as the principal mechanism used to manage aggregate demand. Hence, though initially the Obama administration did achieve a significant and effective fiscal stimulus in the immediate aftermath of the global financial crisis, subsequent management of aggregate demand has been mainly the province of the Fed.

In the Eurozone, the weak confederal structure, with only limited federal powers at the centre, has led to informal, unconstitutional (outside EU treaties) structures and procedures being used. This has led to a lack of transparency and democratic accountability. In relation to the control of the financial sector, the split between the role of the ECB and that of the Eurozone national central banks and national governments has led to a slow resolution of the toxic debt problems of some of the national banks, associated with the damaging impact of the global financial crisis on the EU/EZ financial and banking sectors – and, ultimately, the economic foregone output and the social deprivation. The difficulties arising from over-reliance on the monetary policy of the ECB to manage appropriately aggregate demand, has been worsened by the austerity imposed (via the fiscal compact) on Eurozone countries, promulgated via the unconstitutional Eurogroup and its imposed 'executive federalism'.

By examining the policy actions of the Federal Reserve and the ECB the study has thrown light on the variable impacts of the differing options available to central banks in influencing the behaviour of the financial sector in modern, inter-connected economies. Overall, the evolution of the influence of central banks around the world raises serious political as well as economic concerns and there are democratic implications to be considered insofar as central banks are allowed to operate as independent technocratic entities. These problems have been illuminated by our consideration in this report of the issues raised by an evolving confederal structure, with a new 'quasi-federal' central bank. The political tensions generated following the global financial crisis within the Eurozone have proved a valuable case study of a political and economic system in transition (albeit a lengthy one) from confederalism to federalism.

We examine critically the Eurozone's reactions to the global financial crisis and note design flaws in the original implementation of the Euro as well as the architecture of the European Central Bank and EU executive agencies. The contrast with the US shows that recovery there, while sub-optimal, was better than the EZ's, principally because the US has a full set of federal government institutions. The EZ never knew how to attain similar federal institutions, even though the Euro is a public federal responsibility. We argue that, within the context of a community of laws, a number of institutions have to progress to proper federal agencies and that this process should be accompanied by greater democratic accountability if trust in, and legitimacy of, those institutions is to be assured.

Looking ahead to further research we suggest that the connections between the behaviour of the financial sector and the real economy are complex and unlikely to be satisfactorily explained by the current set of econometric models. The jargon of quantitative easing signals the shortcomings of existing arrangements, themselves an ad hoc adaptation to crisis conditions. In this respect we look to using a broader range of theoretical-economic approaches and the bringing in of sociological and political theoretical insights, especially a wider comparative investigation of federal arrangements.

Chapter 1
Federalism and Central Banks

A federal central bank is something of a misnomer. A central bank belonging to a unitary state is not misnamed. Apart from being placed at the heart of state institutions, a central bank itself creates the conditions that allow the centralization of power within the state. A federal state, by contrast, seeks both to bind together its constituent political units through its central institutions and also to devolve political power downwards to its federated states, its regions and local communities.

A federal central bank is not a stable entity. Over the long *durée* it changes its form and functions, usually in response to political and economic crises and the corresponding forces these unleash. At the present time both the US Federal

Reserve and the European Central Bank are undergoing a legitimacy crisis, mainly because they are carrying out emergency functions not previously envisaged in their legislated mandates. Immediate credit easing was the correct response when the liquidity crisis reached its height in 2008, but as a near-permanent response to a recession triggered by a banking failure it was inadequate to the problems faced in the real economy of goods and labour. Publics are quite within their democratic rights to think that central banks have exceeded their legislated powers and that they have engineered some perverse outcomes. In addition, they have been unable, through monetary policy alone, to restore the US and European economies to good health, now ten years after the start of the global financial crisis.

The future of federal central banks therefore is very much open to change and reform. In contemplating this we first of all identify the sources of instability which any longer-term view shows to be always in play.

1.1 Federalism and Confederalism

A federal political system in theory devolves competences and political functions from its apex downwards to the base and, again in theory, this hierarchy is integrated through a rule-setting democratic constitution. That said however, there is an inherent tension between the political apex, which accumulates powers functional to a territorial state, and the expectation that self-determination should operate at all possible levels.

Historically, most federal political systems develop from a confederation. This is true of Switzerland, Germany, and the United States. Federation of more or less autonomous states is usually a matter of exigency and emergency. Switzerland's religiously differentiated cantons were fused together by Napoleonic decree – federation from above. The United States fought a war of liberation and was forced into federation by the pressing danger[1] of external foreign powers. Germany's federation under Bismarck was a result of foreign wars and aggressive statecraft. The legacy of confederation, however, does not fade away. In Switzerland democracy flows upwards from municipalities and cantons. Bavaria, still the Free State of Bavaria, has continuously threatened and feigned its own autonomy, and no one needs reminding of the American Civil War and the ideological residue of the confederacy.

The European Union is principally to be regarded as a 'confederation of nation-states', tending toward the direction of federation. However, it is, in practice, an amalgam of inter-governmental, confederal, and federal governance elements. As a confederation, the EU defines itself as a 'Community of Laws', a 'Rechtsgemeinschaft', 'Communauté Juridique'. This is a unique and sophisticated way of negotiating the transition from warring states (Europe's own civil wars of the 20th century) to a confederation, in which national state autonomy of laws is gradually modified in the direction of integration. Autonomous national states agree to pooling aspects of their state sovereignty through treaties, and they agree to the governance of specific supranational institutions.

The UK's notified withdrawal shows that the EU remains a confederation of states (though following the Lisbon Treaty of 2009 Article 50 made withdrawal from the Union more punitive). A true federal state exercises a legitimate monopoly of violence within a territorially bounded geographical entity – to use Max Weber's realist definition of a state. It has to defend its borders and therefore it requires a defence force and a defined foreign policy, to think for example of Switzerland.

The European Union, until very recently, has not been forced into becoming a federal state. As a 'protectorate' of the United States, it never seriously had to consider defending its external borders. The Schengen agreement is very much a product of a community of laws, agreed between member states. Without a European army or an effective foreign policy, it is powerless in the face of aggressive foreign powers or large-scale movements of people caused by political instability and war in its 'near abroad'.[2]

As regards this study, creating a central bank within the EU, is seen as an important step in building *towards* a federal state with a common currency. This was the intention of President Mitterrand and Chancellor Kohl's agreement in 1989/1990 to create a common currency and a corresponding central bank, via the establishment of an Economic and Monetary Union. Their decision, often seen as politically contingent, in fact accurately reflected the shifts in the political geography of Europe as Germany re-united; Eastern bloc countries sought accession to the European Union; Russia was no longer an overwhelming external threat; and France, as ever, wanted a 'deepening' of the EU around the Franco-German axis. These geopolitical realities are intensifying, especially with the potential end of Atlanticism as America signals its withdrawal from a multilateral political and economic system.

Although the gradual creation of the European Community was understood as the solution to ending military conflict between European powers and cementing unity among the Member States, nation-state rivalry within the EU has become active again. The expansion of the EU to the East has brought in nation states less enthusiastic about democratic solidarity and more concerned with transactional advantage and the maintenance of their own newly found sovereignty.

Southern European states feel their interests are under-represented within EU institutions. These tensions still have to be played out through the politics of EU federation.

1.2 Central Banks

The institutional design of central banks is always subject to change. In the present period central banks have regularised 'unconventional monetary policy' and this has turned upside down their mode of operation prior to the global financial crisis (GFC). Today, central banks in effect monetize state and corporate debt, determine long term interest rates through massive bond buying programmes, deliberately seek to influence market allocation decisions, indirectly affect fiscal expenditures in selected area, and – despite defined legal remits – have expanded their brief to take on effective governmental responsibility for growth, unemployment and productivity; and last but not least, macroprudential regulation. Prior to the GFC central banks were given the narrow task, independent of government, of maintaining price stability and the soundness of the financial system.

The ECB was founded with the primary brief to issue a new currency and maintain its soundness through the exercise of specific monetary policies. Since 2007 it has creatively, and massively, adapted to the challenges thrown up by the greatest financial crash since 1929. There is not much of the original design left in the face of emergency reactions and ad hoc experimentation, which have generated huge political tensions within member countries of the EU.

Central banks in the US are a lesson in change. Alexander Hamilton's Bank of the United States (1791) monetized the debts of the individual states through issuing new scrip and assured the credit worthiness of US debt, it established and minted a national currency, and it supported the expansion of manufacturing. The Bank of United States was an exercise in state-building, charged by George Washington and James Madison to bind together the individual states and charged by Congress to support the economy. Under the political leadership of the confederal Thomas Jefferson its charter was not renewed in 1810. The same dynamic was played out in 1832 with the abolition of the Second Bank of the United States by Andrew Jackson. The foundation of the Federal Reserve System in 1913 was an attempt, only partially successful, to recognize the differing needs of the regions and to regularize the banking system from the centre. Populism, then as now, is no friend of a central bank.

While we are encouraged to regard a nation's central bank as immutable and a pillar of solidity, dynamic capitalist countries generate strong political and economic forces that impact on central banks and force periodic and profound changes upon them. In particular, these conflicting pressures at times of crisis are transmitted through the central bank, like no other government institution. We have been tutored to perceive a central bank as independent of government and freed from direct democratic control, but despite this it still remains the object of major political pressures.

1.3 Two Pressure Points

Very briefly, we point to two features. Most federal countries are large, and often continental, in size. They contain very different economic regions whose needs have no necessary harmonization or convergence. The political bitterness that inflames debates in the US is grounded historically in the midwestern and farming states that demand cheap credit, the western states that thrive on plentiful credit and the northeast that extracts a premium from tight credit. The European Union's glaring problem is the divide between its northern and southern economic regions. The Eurozone currency area with its associated bank lending has turned southern European nations into debtors, with northern European creditor countries prescribing common economic policies. Federal central banks cannot by themselves solve this problem, since their central mode of operation is monetary policy, which is macro in its effects and by its nature not attuned to regional disparities. Current orthodoxy is based on monetary macroeconomics with fiscal interventions considered undesirable. This places federal central banks in a difficult situation, for they are still expected to ameliorate disparities. The Federal Reserve System of 1913 had a deliberate decentralization built into it to address regional particularities. Early blueprints for a Euro currency included a regional policy as an adjunct to federalization. A Federal Trust paper by Magnifico and Williamson, in 1972, specifically identified the danger of premature monetary integration leading to regional problems taking the place of balance of payment problems (which become intractable within a common currency area).[3]

The other pressure point is the payment systems. Central banks are ultimately responsible for the functioning of these, yet at the same time these are platforms for every kind of banking and transactional exchange. Central banks have been to the fore in creating and coordinating these, making them more universal, more accessible and cheaper to use. But when banking crises and associated liquidity problems blow up, it is the central bank that is forced, often reluctantly, to restore some kind of normality. The global financial crisis came out of unmonitored developments in the payment system, a process of financial rationalization, seemingly unstoppable, and is reckoned, by some, to be the likely cause of the next financial crisis. The subject is technical and usually overlooked.

Responsibility for the payment system is particular vulnerability for central banks. Financial and money markets have an autonomy of their own, especially when they are allowed to innovate without hindrance. But all transactions are carried out in national or federal currencies – the US dollar, the Euro, the renminbi. Currencies are public goods and central banks have to maintain the standing and reliability of a currency; hence the obligation in most central bank mandates to maintain the *soundness* of the money system. The current controversies and intellectual confusion over the role and function of central banks are traceable back to the dual function of a public institution facilitating unconstrained money markets.

1.4 Federal Democracy

This brings us to federal democracy and the principle of self-determination at all levels of a federal political system. There is a reasonable expectation that a *federal* central bank should act in the interests of all its constituent parts. This is countermanded by the reality that a federal central bank is a suprastate/supranational government agency, at one remove from executive power. It issues a common currency and operates a common monetary policy across a federal territory, and it is very much determined by this functionality. In this sense it is a non-discerning part of a centralizing executive; an 'encroachment' of power that George Washington (in offering himself to the electors for a second presidential term) warned, tended to 'despotism'.[4]

John Pinder has sought to square the circle of the conflicting demands, calling for democratization of federal institutions.[5] A European currency and central bank is a necessary part of executive power, required for the beneficial economic integration of European states. But, he argued, it should be democratically accountable to a European parliament, and its mandate is given by the legislature and overseen by a supreme court. We will be showing in this report that the ECB is more executive in its use of discretionary power than democratic in Pinder's sense. This throws up a complex problem of how the democratization of the ECB and EMU should proceed.

Max Weber in his political writings of the day supported a German federation. The major problem he identified was Prussia's dominance and its control of the Bismarckian federal state through the Prussian upper house.[6] The solution? Democratization of the constitution, universal and equal franchise, and competing political parties operating across the political units of the federation. By analogy what is the solution when economic power is concentrated in one executive federal institution and is seen to favour one part or region of a confederation over others?

Jeffersonian democracy would have individual states retain as much power as is not ceded to the federal level. With the expansion of the franchise from property-owners to all male adults, the line between deliberative assemblies of farmers and businessmen to that of populist campaigns and oratorical leaders has been crossed. Simplification of economic grievance and injustice is now a powerful force in populist politics. Intermediating civic institutions – representative democracy – has now become seriously pressured by populist outrage on one side and federal presumption or *Willkür* on the other.

Federal Central Banks

There are no easy answers to the dilemma of self-determination and executive power. In 1998 the Canadian Supreme Court in ruling on the issue of provincial self-determination held that there were four principles that had to be respected equally: Federalism, Democracy, the Constitution and Law.[7] There are no easy compatibilities, even for a sophisticated federal system. Federal central banks have escaped such rigorous and principled examination, adopting as they have, in the present era, legalistic justification buttressed by economic doctrines whose principles of equity are not self-evident.

What follows is an attempt to unpick some of these issues, and to assess the performance of the Federal Reserve and the European Central Bank according to federalist principles.

Notes

1. Gordon White, *Empire of Liberty. A History of the Early Republic 1789-1815* (Oxford University Press, 2009). The argument is the guarantee of liberty vs the expression of liberty.
2. Monnet's original vision of the Union included a defence force. See John Pinder, 'Federal democracy in a federal Europe', in *Federal Democracies*, eds. Michael Burgess and Alain-G. Gagnon (Routledge, 2010), p. 256.
3. G. Magnifico and J. Williamson, *European Monetary Integration*, Federal Trust for Education and Research (1972).
4. Gore Vidal, *Inventing A Nation* (Yale University Press, 2003), p. 125; the modern version is the critique of executive federalism. Donald Smiley has attacked this for a) undue secrecy in management of public affairs, b) low level of citizen involvement, c) public servants made unaccountable to legislatures, d) obstacles to public examination of government policies, e) augments government interventions, e) produces unresolved conflicts of interests through its decisions. See *Federal Democracies*, ed. M. Burgess and A. Gagnon (Routledge 2010), p. 236.

5.   John Pinder, 'Federal democracy in a federal Europe', in *Federal Democracies*, ed. Burgess and Gagnon.

6.   Max Weber, 'Parliament and Government in Germany under a New Political Order', in *Weber. Political Writings*, ed Peter Lassman and Ronald Speirs (Cambridge University Press, 1994), pp. 130-271. One of the main objects of Weber's critique was bureaucracy and officialdom. If one was to work through Weber's critique today, its object would be technocratic officialdom.

7.   Supreme Court of Canada, 'Reference re the Succession of Quebec', tabled August 1998. Cited in *Federal Democracies*, ed. Burgess and Gagnon, p. 14.

Chapter 2
Historical Background

2.1 United States: Evolution and Regression of the Federal Reserve

The modern central bank is, to a significant extent, the product of Franklin D. Roosevelt's reform of American banking and the Bretton Woods agreement of 1944, stabilising the open economic trading environment following the 1930s protectionism. John Maynard Keynes and Harry Dexter White saw the priority as the international system whose reform would lead to an open trading system with built-in regulators for currency imbalances. It is worth re-capitulating its basic architecture since its legacy is more than ever relevant – even though its salient features have mostly been forgotten. Despite the monetarist re-orientation starting in the 1980s, the public image of a central bank today still draws on this legacy: a central bank discreet and in the background of economic policy, and authoritative and competent in its handling of government debt, exchange rate moves, and bank regulation. This is still the public's understanding of 'sound money'.

We can simplify the historical phases of the US Federal Reserve by first considering the problems the country faced and secondly the solutions arrived at. Then we can gain a picture of the changes to the institutional architecture. This encompasses the executive branch of government, Congress representing the separate states and their regional groupings, and the judiciary. We should not overly focus on central banks, because at the executive and administrative level Treasuries or Finance Ministries can make a better claim to priority.

The Federal Reserve System, founded in 1913, was the response to agricultural depression which had been chronic since the 1890s and there was a major banking crisis in 1907. The other far better-known crisis was the Great Crash of 1929 and the succeeding depression. When President Roosevelt entered office in March 1933, a quarter of the country's banks had closed and credit to commerce had shrunk from $50 (in 1928) to $30 billion. Overdrafts and loans to industry, businessmen and farmers were withdrawn. Farmer were made destitute, and large industries were shut down. Wages went unpaid. A quarter of the workforce was unemployed. Industrial output fell by half, prices dropped by 30% and national income shrank from $100 to $55 billion.[1]

The problem was roughly the same in both episodes. From the farmers' perspective, agricultural prices were too low and the price of farm mortgages and temporary credit for seasonal workers was too high. The banking failures of 1907 and 1929 had devastating consequences for farmers, reducing them to tenant penury. America was much more of a manufacturing economy by 1929, and the role of finance in the capitalist economy was far more pivotal; what J.M. Keynes referred to as 'monetary production economy'.[2] Bank failures led directly to bankruptcies and shuttering of firms in the real economy.

The main driver of political and banking reform was agrarian populism. This movement almost delivered William Jennings Bryan to the White House as the Democratic presidential nominee in 1908. His slogan was an attack against 'money power'. His oratorical gifts were aimed at the East Coast and Wall Street banks, which he denounced tying credit to the gold standard. His movement supported a silver standard and distributing silver to citizens (a direct form of QE). The intention was to introduce more liquidity into the economy so bidding up the price of commodities in manufacturing and farming. (Again, echoes of QE in the face of stubborn deflation.) Banking crises deflated the value of money and purchasing power, though debt repayments remained at ex ante values. Farmers lost their land and livelihood. The pattern repeated after 1929 and President Roosevelt genuinely feared a farmers' revolution throughout 1933.

Bryan never made it to the Presidency but he certainly changed the Democrats economic programme. (He was eventually coopted in the administration of Woodrow Wilson in 1913 as Secretary of State.) The foundation of the Federal Reserve System in 1913 was the long overdue solution to the perpetual story of widespread bank failures. A banking commission had been set up in 1907 and Woodrow Wilson made reform part of his electoral programme. Paul Warburg, an emigrant from the Hamburg finance house of that name, was a member of the commission and argued for a Bank of England solution. At a time of crisis the central bank gives any amount liquidity in exchange for good sound bills – and in practice not so sound bills. By this mechanism, commercial and private banks would not have to keep large reserves, so restricting their ability to lend.

To Warburg's intense frustration this solution was not adopted. Rationalism had to give way to *Interessenpolitik*. This is something of a universal rule, though is obscured today by economists adopting the positions of major interests. Bryan as well as Senator Carter Glass (Dem. Virginia) pushed hard for reform, but were of course countered by both Democratic and Republican opposition in the North East, which adhered to the gold standard and laissez faire. The populist position repeated the Jeffersonian mantra of not passing powers upwards to federal agencies in Washington. In addition the banking commission set up to produce reforms was populated with private bankers who resisted the idea that a central, federal bank should regulate their reserves, interest rates, and issue of currency and credit. This is well recounted in the books respectively by Ahamed and Lowenstein. [3]

The resultant solution was a political compromise. President Wilson did get to appoint the chairman and deputy to the Federal Board, sited in Washington. But the head of the Federal Board could be outmanoeuvred in practice by powerful federal bank chairs, in particular the New York Fed (which was overwhelmingly important for capital markets). The 1913 scheme was something less than a central bank but one that distributed private/commercial bank reserves around the major regions of the United States. Nine regional federal banks were created (the regions were selected by the Treasury and Agriculture Secretaries) and their boards were composed of private bankers. The Federal Reserve Banks had to keep

40% reserves (specie, coin and greenbacks) and in emergency these were physically transported to the points of need. The system created a new architecture, but a faulty one. The regionalism, imposed by Treasury Secretary William McAdoo, was a welcome acknowledgement that different economic areas were not congruent with state boundaries. They allowed, in theory, a representation of the major regions, even though in practice each regional board went its own way. In addition, there was no effective link up between the Federal Reserve and the U.S. Treasury. Government money creation and borrowing could not be transferred across to the Federal Reserve, dominated as it was by the mindset of private bankers. McAdoo, in response, would arbitrarily simply transfer gold reserves to regional federal banks as he thought fit.

The Federal Reserve System failed in almost every respect during the Great Crash. As Paul Warburg feared, in a financial panic the Federal Reserve Banks hoarded their reserves and failed to alleviate problems at the point of greatest need. What had pointedly been refused was the idea that a central bank could ease the situation, at will, through issuing credit notes. Although a federal open market committee was established in 1923, it was barely used. In matters of economic dogma, many of the Federal Reserve Banks adhered to the 'real bills' doctrine, which was inherently deflationary and aligned to the commodity theory of money. In the politics of money the crucial issue is what secures the value of a currency – with land, physical goods and commodities, gold, and silver all having their political advocates – and economic beneficiaries.

President Roosevelt in almost all respects bypassed the Federal Reserve System and moved directly to wholesale reform of the banks putting an Emergency Banking Act through Congress in one day. Some thousands of insolvent banks were closed down or forced to merge. Existing banks were re-capitalised through the Reconstruction Finance Corporation, which was a federal agency and major engine of the New Deal. The Federal Deposit Insurance Scheme obligated all participating banks to be subject to close supervision, and it was run out of the Reconstruction Corporation.

It was only after a reforming chair (Marriner Eccles) of the Federal Reserve Board had been put in place that banks were forcibly made to join the Federal Reserve System, in 1936. The Regional Federal Banks, apart from being jointly owned by private banks, had considerable autonomy in decision making, to which the main Board had only veto rights. Eccles' Federal Reserve Board would 'introduce certain attributes of a real central bank capable of energetic and positive action'. This demanded a transfer of authority and responsibility to the Federal Board in Washington.[4] Eccles' justification for this was that 'laissez faire in banking and the attainment of business stability are incompatible. If variations in the supply of money are to be compensatory and corrective rather than inflammatory and intensifying, there must be conscious and deliberate control'. The new Act finally dispatched the 'real bills' doctrine that only trade assets were eligible for re-discounting. A range of bank assets including mortgages, could now be exchanged for Federal Reserve notes.

Roosevelt's other momentous decision was to break the fixed price link of the dollar to gold. This effectively ended the gold standard regime, negated the power of New York investment banks and their links to the City of London. It also placed the United States on a fiat currency and placed the domestic economy above the international banking system. The outrage among bankers was incandescent. Roosevelt knew what he was up against, as he wrote to his confidant Colonel House: 'The real truth of the matter is, as you and I know, that a financial element in the larger centers has owned the Government ever since the days of Andrew Jackson – and I am not wholly excepting the Administration of W.W. The country is going through a repetition of Jackson's fight with the Bank of the United States – only on a far bigger and broader basis.'[5] In making the US dollar non-convertible against gold (leading to a major devaluation of the dollar against the international standard of gold) he used an Act of Congress, the Agricultural Amendment Act.

The evolution of central banks has been driven by financial crashes and bank panics; however, in federal constitutions reform has to proceed according to the law, and executive decisions can be revoked, or endorsed, by a supreme court. This is to be reminded of the Canadian Supreme Court ruling (end of Chapter 1) that Law, Constitution, Democracy and Federalism all have to be respected. Roosevelt was very much aware of this and he ensured that the major advances in federal government were legal and were approved by Congress.

It was an old Civil War Act that gave the President discretionary power to issue currency and notes. At that time (1933) the Federal Board was refusing to buy $3 billion from the US Treasury. Roosevelt, in threatening a clear abuse of executive power, forced the Federal Board to expand its balance sheet and emit credit. With these moves a federal central bank came of age. The currency was placed on a fiat basis, and the Federal Reserve was nominally in charge of the supply of money and credit. The controlling institution was the Treasury, the fiscal core of any state. It decided how much sovereign debt it would issue, how much the banks and the Federal Reserve would buy, and at what rate of interest.

Through the Bretton Woods agreement of 1944 this arrangement was rolled out by all participating countries. Bretton Woods and the IMF introduced tight fiscal and monetary discipline in a world of fixed exchange rates. Autonomy of interest rate setting and credit issuance in all these countries came under Treasury control – and lasted until the 1970s. Democratic accountability proceeded through parliaments from which Treasuries received their electoral mandate and day to day accountability. Internationally, agreement with Bretton Woods was legislated through state treaties. This was a functional architecture, replicated on an international scale (and it will be seen how Nixon's imperial presidency undermined this architecture). It has, of course, been noted that Bretton Woods was politically overseen by Treasury Secretary Morgenthau whose hatred of and disgust with the banks knew no bounds. Roosevelt's federal banking reforms and Bretton Woods were effected without the presence of bankers, an example of making full unobstructed use of a crisis, *pace* Treasury Secretary Geithner.[6]

Clearly there was an element of retrospective legitimation of measures that had arisen due to emergency and exigency (both the Depression and the postwar indebtedness of European nations). Any executive overreach was, however, in the democratic spirit of the age following 1945, brought within legislative oversight and democratic accountability of newly empowered citizen nations.

Under a Federal Reserve – Treasury agreement in April 1951, the Federal Reserve won the right to set the federal interest rate and, directly related to that, the amount and type (long and short) of Treasury bonds it bought. Prior to that, the Treasury Secretary effectively ordered the Federal Reserve Banks to buy treasuries of his determining. This created a low interest regime and a flat yield curve (i.e. no significance difference in the yield on short and long-term bonds).[7] This is a reminder that all central banks start out as bankers to the state, and they retain or revive this function whenever emergencies strike, which usually come about by paying for wars or financial crises.

McChesney Martin who was leading the Federal Reserve in 1951 (and supported by the previous chair Marriner Eccles) objected to subsidizing the borrowing needs of the United States Treasury. These needs had arisen because the demand of US dollars in the post-1945 world was immense and the US willingly accommodated this demand through its expenditure at home and abroad and its lending policies to foreign governments. It was unique in not having to follow the rules agreed at Bretton Woods. It was the major banker to the International Money Fund and effectively the US dollar was the new currency standard. In the original Bretton Woods scheme the underlying reserve money of all central banks was intended to be a composite currency, 'bancor'. But since the US had the lion's share of gold (which had again become the reference price for the dollar) and since it was the world's creditor, bancor was overridden by the mighty dollar. Keynes's rationalism succumbing to the force majeure of Harry Dexter White.[8]

In Europe the only political leader to challenge what became known as the dollar's 'exorbitant privilege' was President de Gaulle in the late 1950s. The US was emitting so many dollars into the international system that at some point its price would fall against gold. De Gaulle ordered the Banque de France to increase its gold reserves. Though a national move, not copied elsewhere,[9] this was the first step in motivating the European movement in thinking about a European currency independent of the US dollar.

Despite de Gaulle's doubts about the sustainability of the value of the dollar, the US – under IMF rules – continued to swap dollars for gold. However, such was the domestic and foreign (war) expenditures of the US in the 1960s that in 1971 President Nixon shut the 'gold window'. The world moved to floating exchange rates with no one anchor of value. The US Treasury was conspicuous in its inability or reluctance to put in place a reformed international system, one also de-stabilised by the oil price hikes. The situation was compounded by the 'Reagonomics' of the 1980s that flagrantly disregarded the growing gap between unconstrained expenditure and insufficient taxation; a gap filled by the issuing of ever more US treasuries. This trajectory tops out with the Chinese as the eager buyer of trillions of dollars worth of US treasuries, so financing a geopolitical world of America's choosing.

This was the international backdrop which, in its geopolitical repercussions, was increasing the pressure for some kind of European currency able to stand on its own alongside the US dollar.

2.2 EU and Eurozone

Turning to the foundation of the ECB, how does the story compare? The first thing to note is that the United States offers no clear paradigm, or rather, institutional designs are subject to periodic intervention and changing political currents. Canada with its four enunciated principles would be a better guide, other than this was a federal constitution imposed from above (in 1867) with the watchword 'peace, order and government'. The United States was a self-created constitution with federal executive powers always in conflict with the Jeffersonian maxim of citizen autonomy. The circumstances of foundation of confederalism or federalism are determinative but not necessarily ordering.

That said, the Europeans were in a position to learn the lessons of the history of the Federal Reserve and to give considerable thought to the design of common currency with its own issuing bank. As will be seen in next section there were a number blueprints, which are worth evaluating from an *ex ante* viewpoint. It does not take too much intellectual acumen to see *retrospectively* how these plans foundered in the face of the realities of political and financial economy, most obviously the GFC. Yet we can adjudge the various plans in terms of what elements they could have been expected to include.

Despite the fluctuations in the history of federal central banking, there are core elements always in play and their sequencing is critical. For example, and very briefly, under Bismarck the second German Empire (founded 1871) established a common currency (the Reichsmark) and a central bank (Reichsbank) in a newly constituted federal political system. The earlier crucially formative stage in this process was the North German Customs Union, which by 1840 had abolished tariffs across numerous state borders, so facilitating economic integration and the growth of trade. The sequence, or better still, the path dependency is: customs union, political federation, fiscal federation, common currency and central bank (and in the German case the establishment of regional banks fostered by the Reichsbank).

Schematically – with empirical variation removed – the United States's path dependency is: political confederation, customs union, political federation (1864), permanent central bank (1913) with a common currency only becoming widely accessible in 1930s alongside fiscal federalism.

In both the above cases political federation was achieved through war and subjugation (and included war budgets and state debt). That was not an 'option' for the European Union which was founded on the premise of peaceful integration.

The path dependency of Europe is: customs union, political confederation, single market (an enhanced customs union), common currency and central bank. Creating a common currency and central bank prior to and without political and fiscal federation introduces a novel path dependency. Did the ex ante plans sufficiently anticipate the potential problems?

2.3 Early EMU Initiatives

The context within which these early schemes and plans were conceived was the collapse of the Bretton Woods system. This unleashed several degrees of disorder. There was no longer a fixed anchor of currency exchange rates and instead, in Europe, each country experienced volatility in the value of its national currency. In addition, the discipline on domestic economies broke down. Inflationary pressures could be alleviated through devaluation, which in the previous rule bound universe of the IMF was only possible under strict rules and penalties. This new instability set the terms for the ensuing path dependency.

European Monetary Integration, put together by Dr G. Magnifico and Prof J. Williamson in 1972 following wide consultation with business, finance, politicians and officials, opted for the revolutionary step of full monetary union managed by a single central bank system.[10] This seized the nettle of fluctuating exchange rates. They argued that not only would exchange risk be reduced (including the subsidy paid by national central banks to currency speculation) but that a) increased capital mobility would offset balance of payment problems, b) reserves would be pooled giving stability to the currency they termed the Europa, c) it opened the way to re-establishing control of Europe-wide monetary conditions.

The Report looked forward to a European (central) Bank. Initially, this would have to establish the credibility of the Europa as a stable reserve currency, able to determine its value against SDRs and gold (this was a residual belief in the Bretton Woods scheme). When established, it assumed that taxes would be paid in Europas (so establishing its chartal status as money) and that it would act as a clearing house for pan European transactions (a core function of a central bank). The final stages would see public bodies issuing Europa-denominated bonds, including national debt of member states, and acting as a market maker in Europa-denominated Treasury bills; finally, assuming the responsibility as the lender of last resort.

The Report was aiming for a proper, full-functioning central bank, equivalent to the Federal Reserve. The authors did anticipate certain problems that could or would occur along their favoured path. Monetary union and monetary policy would not displace the need for Europe-wide fiscal policy, wage policy, planning and regional policy. In particular the report highlighted the danger of substituting regional disparities for the endemic balance of payment problems. By binding all of the national currencies into one currency, less competitive economies would be unable to depreciate their currency to restore competitive prices for their exports. Different levels of competitiveness reflected the uneven development of economies (in particular northern Europe compared to the south). Therefore it was necessary, they argued, to implement an effective regional policy to allow convergence. Failure to appreciate these dangers, they noted, could lead to the destruction of the monetary union.[11]

The question left unanswered at this early point was what political authority would oversee the central bank as well as the regional and fiscal policies. The implicit suggestion is that political federation, with federal state institutions, would have to occur at some point. The priority in 1972, however, was to counter the collapse of the Bretton Woods system.

Another report, the Werner Report, was official and represented a significant step in the evolution of the European Union's plans to establish an economic and monetary union (EMU). In 1969, the heads of state or government defined a new objective of European integration: economic and monetary union. A group headed by Pierre Werner, Prime Minister of Luxembourg, drafted a report which envisaged the achievement of full economic and monetary union within 10 years according to a plan in several stages. It was the beginning of the drive to achieve full economic and monetary integration within the EEC. The integration would be marked by the full liberalisation of capital movements within the EEC area; the full convertibility of Member States' currencies, and the irrevocable fixing of exchange rates between the countries.

But it was the disruption caused by the collapse of the Bretton Woods system and the ensuing wave of instability in respect of foreign exchange operations that meant that the initial plans for the EMU were brought to an abrupt halt. It was seven years before the idea of EMU was resuscitated at a Brussels summit meeting in 1978. The need for a European plan had not gone away, especially as it became apparent that no Bretton Woods version 2 would be forthcoming.

It was agreed to create a European Monetary System (EMS). The EMS – though the official EU history mis-records the key element – comprised the Exchange Rate Mechanism, which the UK half-joined, and the *European Monetary Fund* (EMF).[12] As its name suggests it was a European equivalent of the IMF, and one that re-visited the scheme envisaged by Keynes. The fund would be a pooling of European central bank reserves. These could be drawn upon to ameliorate the economic dislocations attendant on a failure of any national currency to stay within the fixed rate bands.

National exchange rates were based on central rates against the European Currency Unit (ECU). This was a weighted average of the participating currencies, and fluctuations of the individual national bilateral rates had to be kept within 2.25 % either side of the central rates expressed in ECU, with the exception of the Italian lira which was permitted a margin of 6%.

The politics of what happened next were unfortunate. The EMF was consigned to history by Germany, despite the system having been designed principally by Horst Schulman (who was a senior official of the EU Commission and subsequently became State Secretary in the German government). Again, we have to go back to Keynes to see why this was a retrograde step. Without a fund there was no buffering mechanism to absorb exogenous or domestic shocks to member countries' economies. Also, rather like the US currency dominance of the IMF, Germany as the leading economy, would effectively create a D-Mark zone. It was for this reason that the Labour government, under the advice of Chancellor Denis Healey, declined to join the ERM scheme. Germany was keen to preserve a fixed rate currency union that cemented its competitive advantages against other member states, and it consistently refused to adapt these rates to allow for a phased revaluation of the DM.

The UK did eventually join the ERM in 1990, under the Conservatives, principally as a means of constraining inflation, but at a clearly unsustainable parity of 2.95 DM to the pound, only to crash out two years later, in 1992, on what became known as Black Wednesday. Ironically, in 1993, the banding was expanded to 15% to accommodate the problems of the French franc.[13]

Notwithstanding the relative success of the ERM in stabilising exchange rates, from 1979 to 1989 with the impending development of the 'Single Market' programme there were concerns that further integration was required. This need was highlighted by the inability to achieve full exploitation of an internal market, given the relatively high transaction costs linked to currency conversion and the uncertainties linked to exchange rate fluctuations however constrained.

Taking stock of these hesitant steps, we can ask whether the design and planning of a European Monetary System was fully aware of the dangers that lay ahead. The Werner report saw the matter as one of reaching integration through the convergence of European national currencies. Fluctuating exchange rates, also have to be seen in the light of the massive Eurodollar market, offshore from the United States. This enabled currency speculation and increased volatility.

That noted, Europe could not be said to be in an emergency situation, but rather was simply harassed by exchange markets. Europe lacked its own Hamiltonian founding moment and proceeded step by step on a monetary led strategy in place of an overall design that could resist the political contingencies, which came to determine policy.

2.4 The changed political context: Chancellor Kohl and President Mitterrand

In the 1980s Germany was far less keen on the idea of EMU than the French political class and certainly less so than the UK. However, in 1989, a conjunction of two major European political events: the pressure from France to move forward on EMU and simultaneously the proposed unification of West and East Germany, created a major dilemma.

France and the UK were both seriously concerned about the prospect of a unified Germany becoming the dominant economic and political force within the EU. The obvious commitment of Chancellor Kohl to push forward rapidly with a programme to unite West and East Germany, while at the same time blocking the wider integration of the EU under EMU, apparently left Mitterrand incandescent with rage. He issued an ultimatum to Kohl that he would only support German unification if Germany supported substantial progress on EMU.[14]

Faced with opposition from France and the UK, Kohl agreed to allow progress on EMU. The issue was then shifted down to a political process involving Jacques Delors the French President of the European Commission and Otto Pöhl, President of the Bundesbank. The trade-off agreed between Pöhl, himself very reluctant to agree an EMU which would damage the financial discipline of Germany, and Delors emerged in the form of the 1992 Maastricht Treaty.[15] This stipulated strict financial criteria to be observed by member states adhering to EMU and tight stability criteria also for states applying for membership. The criteria were, in themselves unsupported by any economic reasoning, but allowed Germany to accept EMU. Ironically, it was Germany which following the establishment of the Euro in 1998 became the first member state to breach the financial deficit criterion, following the establishment of the Eurozone and the Euro as a common currency for the participating countries.

Given the general reluctance of Germany to surrender 'control' of an independent Eurozone central bank it is not surprising that the model for the ECB is the Bundesbank, together with a tight inflation target.[16] The intention was to make sure that a similar financial rectitude to that which has characterised the post-war Bundesbank was replicated in the operation of the ECB. Until the impact of the GFC this was the case. However, it might be observed that the policy actions of the Bundesbank in Germany were situated in the context of the various democratic government economic and financial policy institutions, not least the Tariff agreements between trade unions and employers.[17] In the case of the Eurozone this democratic governmental nexus is absent.

The French more than any other nation were aware of the pressing need of establishing a European economic and political presence in the face of America's increasing disregard of the rules of the post-war international settlement. Germany, a nation introspectively oriented to its own economic success and comfortable with its Atlanticism, saw little reason to consider the wider geopolitical position of Europe. The belt and braces fastenings of Maastricht offered a re-assurance to the German citizen, but that very inflexibility was to prove economically problematic as an operating construct, once the Euro and the ECB were established in 1998. Subsequent events have indicated the flaws and missing links in the Eurozone construct, and only now, in 2017, is there any serious attempt to provide an improved economic and fiscal architecture to remedy these omissions and lack of democratic control. Again the French appear to be in the vanguard of advocating reform in the Eurozone in order to maintain its legitimacy amongst European citizens.

2.5 EMU in detail

Looking at the evolution of the move to economic and monetary union (EMU) in more detail, in 1989 the Delors

Report proposed to move to full economic and monetary union in three discrete stages. The first stage, full liberalisation of capital movements was implemented by the end of 1990. Allowing the free flow of capital prior to the completion of later stages, may be considered a mistaken path dependency. This freedom was exercised to the detriment of ERM stability in 1992, so much so that the reintroduction of those same capital controls was seriously considered.

The implementation of the second two stages would require a new Treaty, a Treaty on European Union, the so-called Maastricht Treaty, signed in 1992.

- Stage 1 (from 1 July 1990 to 31 December 1993): the free movement of capital between Member States (already agreed and implemented pre-Maastricht);
- Stage 2 (from 1 January 1994 to 31 December 1998): convergence of Member States' economic policies and strengthening of cooperation between Member States' national central banks. The coordination of monetary policies was strengthened by the establishment of the European Monetary Institute (EMI). Its task was to strengthen cooperation between the national central banks and to carry out the necessary preparations for the introduction of the single currency. *The national central banks were also to become independent during this stage*;
- Stage 3 (under way since 1 January 1999 for those countries joining the Eurozone): the gradual introduction of the euro as the single currency of the Member States and the implementation of a common monetary policy under the aegis of the ECB. Transition to the third stage was subject to the achievement of a high degree of durable convergence measured against a number of criteria laid down by the Treaties. The budgetary rules were to become binding and a Member State not complying with them

was likely to face penalties. A single monetary policy was introduced and entrusted to the European System of Central Banks (ESCB), made up of the national central banks and the newly instituted ECB.

The first two stages of EMU have been completed, with all countries participating, including the UK. The third stage is still under way. In principle, *all* EU Member States must join this final stage and therefore adopt the euro (Article 119 TFEU). However, some Member States have not yet fulfilled the convergence criteria. These Member States consequently benefit from a provisional derogation until they are able to join the third stage of EMU.

Convergence here means strict budget rules. The debate in the 1970s was framed differently as one between 'monetary' convergence and 'economic' convergence. One side, predominantly German theorists, argued that only when the very different economies of the Union were more closely aligned, did it make sense to move to monetary union. The 'monetarists' on the other hand argued convergence could be achieved through monetary union. By the 1990s there had been limited progress in economic convergence; most notably the British Treasury conducted a major exercise to show its economy was far from converging and hence its refusal to join the Euro.[18] Budget uniformity according to Maastricht criteria papered over the basic issue of misaligned economies within the monetary union. Both politics and economics overrode Maastricht rules following German unification. Indeed politics overrode the Bundesbank with Kohl decreeing the exchange rate of Ostmark for Deutschmark, against the wishes of Pöhl. And in 1998, as noted, joining together such divergent economies under a common currency made inevitable Germany's own breach of Maastricht budgetary rules.

2.6 Establishment of the ECB

The ECB was established in 1998, following on from the earlier European Monetary Institute (EMI) as indicated above, ready for the formal launch of the Euro in January 1999. Despite the economic disturbances of the 1990s, the aftershock of the collapse of the eastern bloc, the institutions of the EU were adhering to the blueprints of the early 1990s. In the outline that follows it has to be remembered that a unique experiment was underway: the creation of a central bank for a *confederal* political system. As appropriate to a community of laws, it was rules, enshrined in treaties, that were to determine the shape and effectiveness of the ECB. And to anticipate, when the GFC broke it was these rules that both circumscribed and determined the response of the ECB.

Member States who were going to be part of the Eurozone were assessed by the Commission, the Council of Ministers, and the European Parliament – based on detailed reports of the EMI – as to their qualification to be members of the Eurozone. The parameters examined were those encompassed by the Maastricht criteria, i.e. government budget deficit below 3% of GDP; public debt to GDP ratio below 60%, and inflation running at around 2%, *plus* proof of staying within the ERMII exchange rate boundaries, + or – 15%, for a minimum of 2 years.

In practice there was flexibility around these parameters, e.g. the Italian debt to GDP ratio was well above the required 60% at around 100%. Indeed there was some discussion in the European Parliament as to whether this should prevent Italy from becoming a member of the Eurozone. In the end political considerations dictated the final complement of 11 Eurozone members in 1999. (Subsequently, once having been judged to have satisfied the Maastricht criteria, a further 8 member states have joined the Eurozone, taking the membership up to 19 members).

At the same time, in 1998, the 6 members of the ECB Board, including the President and the Vice-President (Netherlands, Belgium, and Luxembourg agreed to have one nominee representing the three countries) were nominated, by the Eurozone countries, and their appointments ratified by the European Parliament (EP), after being interviewed by the EP. There was some resistance in the EP to one country's nominee, but after pressure from that country's MEPs, the appointment of the nominee was ratified. At that time it was not clear that, apart from embarrassment, any objection raised by the EP would have led to the nominee standing down.

At the same time there was considerable discussion within the EP on the specific numerical inflation target, within the overall price stability objective for the ECB. Ultimately the target was fixed as *'an inflation rate in the Eurozone area of below, but close to, 2% over the medium term'*, as measured by the HCIP (Harmonised Index of Consumer Prices).[19]

The Euro would be brought into use simultaneously in all 11 Eurozone countries in January 1999.

2.7 Structure of ECB

Despite its independence, the operations of the ECB are *formally* circumscribed. The ECB Board has six members, the President, the Vice-President and the four other members. Members serve for a non-renewable term of eight years.

It is important to understand that the ECB Board is, by statute, part of the European System of Central Banks

(ESCB). The ESCB includes all of the central banks of the EU and is run by a Governing Council, which comprises the ECB Executive Board and the Governors of the EU national central banks (NCBs).

The governors of the Eurozone central banks are known collectively as the Eurosystem and the Eurosystem is run by a Governing Council comprising the Executive Board members of the ECB and the central bank governors of the 19 countries of the Eurozone.

The Governing Council is responsible, in the context of the relevant TFEU articles, to improve monetary and financial cooperation between the Eurosystem and those EU countries currently outside the Eurozone. However, on issues concerning the Eurozone the NCB members of countries outside the Eurozone do not take part in discussions of ECB policy or decisions applicable within the Eurozone.

The primary objective of the ECB, mandated in Article 2 of the Statute of the ECB, is to maintain price stability within the Eurozone (as defined above). Its basic tasks, set out in Article 3 of the Statute, are to set and implement the monetary policy for the Eurozone; to conduct foreign exchange operations; to take care of the foreign reserves of the Eurosystem banks, and to manage the operation of the financial market infrastructure under the Target 2 payments system and the technical platform for settlement of securities in Europe, i.e. Target 2 securities. The ECB has, under Article 16 of its Statute, the exclusive right to authorise the issuance of euro banknotes. Member states can issue euro coins, but the amount must be authorised by the ECB beforehand.

The ECB is set up to be independent of the Member States and of any attempt to be influenced politically in its decisions. Elaboration of the issue of independence and what exactly is implied is discussed below.

2.8 The Eurozone Group of Finance Ministers and its Secretariat

The governance and administration of the Eurozone, aside from the European System of Central Banks and the ECB, is placed in the hands of the Eurogroup of finance ministers, with occasional summit meetings of the Eurogroup heads of government.

It is important to recognise that this inter-governmental body is only recognised by the TFEU in respect of voting rights over Eurozone issues. According to the Lisbon Treaty (2009) dealing with the Eurogroup, the main task of the Eurogroup is 'to discuss questions related to the specific responsibilities they [the ministers of Eurozone Member States] share with regard to the single currency'. It has no specific legal authority.[20]

There is a European Working Group (EWG) which involves representatives of the Eurogroup finance ministers, the European Commission, and the ECB. The participation of the ECB *could* lead to the Bank influencing decisions outside its policy remit.

The President of the Eurogroup is elected for 2.5 years. However, this role does not imply that the holder will serve the group as such, but will represent the views of his/her own national government. The Eurogroup situation is even more unsatisfactory because of the enhanced role of the Eurogroup following the financial crisis and the various legal measures taken by the EU in relation to macro-economic monitoring and control, as indicated in chapters 6 and 7 below. Effectively, the Eurogroup has a privileged position in that the views of the group have to be taken into account by the Commission and the Council when considering the macro-economic situation of the whole EU.

2.9 Role of the European Parliament

Following the establishment of the ECB, the European Parliament was to receive regular annual reports from the ECB and the President of the ECM appeared regularly before the relevant Committee of the Parliament.

Since the entry into force of the Lisbon Treaty in 2009, the European Parliament has participated as equal co-legislator in the ordinary legislative procedure in establishing detailed rules for multilateral surveillance (Article 121(6) TFEU). This involves, inter alia, the preventive part of the Stability and Growth Pact, as well as more diligent macroeconomic surveillance to prevent harmful imbalances following the financial crisis. The 'six-pack' (see below) strengthened Parliament's role in the economic governance of the EU, in particular through the introduction of the 'European Semester' and the installation of an 'Economic Dialogue'. In addition, Parliament is consulted on the following issues:

- agreements on exchange rates between the euro and non-EU currencies;
- the choice of countries eligible to join the single currency in 1999 and subsequently;
- the appointment of the President, Vice-President and other members of the ECB Executive Board;
- legislation implementing the excessive deficit procedure provided for in the Stability and Growth Pact.

2.10 Structural comparisons of ECB and Federal Reserve

It is possible to summarize succinctly the structure and function of the Federal Reserve. At its base the Federal Reserve Banks are hybrid of private and public institutions, that is, commercial bank representatives sitting on the boards of a public institution. The Chair and Vice-Chair of the Washington Federal Reserve Board are appointed by the President of the United States. The Federal Reserve is accountable twice yearly to Congress, which fixes its mandate. The 1978 Humphrey-Hawkins mandate stipulates that the Fed is to 'maintain long-run growth of the monetary and credit aggregates commensurate with the economy's long run potential to increase production, so as to promote effectively the goals of maximum unemployment, stable prices, and moderate long-term interest rates.'[21] The Fed is embedded into federal government: the executive and legislature. Although Treasury officials no longer have the official right to sit on the Federal Reserve Board, there is of course a fiscal treasury with immense reserves that stands behind the Fed. The Treasury, political and executive in its functioning, determines how much debt is issued. Exactly which institution determines the price of debt is a contentious issue, but in times of financial crisis, it is the Treasury that assumes the dominant role. Ultimately, it is citizen taxation and the power of the federal state that underpins the nation's bank. Despite Hamilton's best efforts, it took over two hundred years to reach this arrangement.

The stand-out difference for Europe is that the European Union is not a federal state. It has many Presidents – of the Parliament, of the Commission, of the Council, of the ECB, of the Eurogroup – but there is no presidential executive leadership. This is simply the difference between a federal and a confederal political system. The other stand-out difference – amazingly usually overlooked – is that the EU and EZ do not have a Treasury. To create, so to speak, the float on which the ECB was launched, national central banks committed a large portion of their reserves to the ECB. Taken with Maastricht criteria, this represented a critical loss of monetary sovereignty by nation states to the new currency and the ECB, without however the ECB achieving an increase in its monetary sovereignty commensurate with the loss experienced at national level. In a financial crisis Treasury and central bank have to work hand in hand, with Treasuries (or Finance Departments) doing the heavy lifting of issuing bonds and altering taxation to cover the chasms of bankrupt banks and deficit state budgets. As already noted this was in the first blueprint of Horst Schulman in the form of the EMF, but the ECB in its compromised design was not given this capacity.

In chapters 6 and 7 we suggest that this was a mistake and that the Maastricht design of EMU has led to a problematic EZ architecture, which is in need of radical reform.

Notes

1. J. K. Galbraith, *The Great Crash 1929* (Hamish Hamilton, 1955), p. 186; Liaquat Ahamed, *The Lords of Finance. 1929, The Great Depression and the Bankers who broke the world* (Penguin, 2009), p. 448.

2. J.M. Keynes, 'A monetary theory of production', reprinted in *Collected Writings* XX1, ed. D. Moggridge (Macmillan, [1933]1973).

3. Roger Lowenstein, *America's Bank. The Epic Struggle to Create the Federal Reserve*, Penguin Press, 2015. Liaquat Ahamed, *The Lords of Finance. 1929, The Great Depression and the Bankers who broke the world* (Penguin, 2009).

4. T. G. Moe, 'Marriner S. Eccles and the 1951 Treasury–Federal Reserve Accord: Lessons for central bank independence', *Norges Banks* (15 May 2014), p. 17.

5. A. Schlesinger, *The Age of Roosevelt* (Heinemann, 1957), p. 239.

6. See Benn Steil, *The Battle for Bretton Woods. John Maynard Keynes and Harry Dexter White and the Making of a New World Order* (Princeton University Press, 2012), p. 13. Morgenthau also blamed the financial crash for the rise of Hitlerism in Germany, the rise of *völkisch* populism fuelled by the failure of

Credit Anstalt and the resulting economic mayhem. This is why an international solution had to be found. The NSDAP's assumption of power was through democratic election. Thereafter Law was not respected, nor did the Bundesbank obey its constitutional mandate. Under the evil genius Dr Hjalmar Schacht the Reichsbank deceived its foreign creditors, cheated German citizens of their purchasing power, and extorted German industry (not without the latter's collusion). This hidden history of the Reichsbank has been revealed by Adam Tooze in his *The Wages of Destruction* (Allen Lane, 2006). It is a history that has haunted the post-war Bundesbank (founded in 1957 in place of the regional banks of the federal German Länder) as much as Weimar inflation and the destruction of the Reichsmark and associated savings in 1948.

7. Morgenthau, and his successors after 1947, ordered the Federal Reserve to intervene in the market for government bonds, whenever the Treasury issued more debt; this was after the Second World War. Allan Meltzer, *History of Federal Reserve, Vol I: 1913-1951* (Chicago: Chicago University Press, 2003), pp. 703-707,737-8. The Fed had to buy bonds to keep the price of them up. This is exactly the same as the massively more extensive programme of asset purchases from 2009 by the Federal Reserve whose purpose was to reduce interest rates. Morgenthau cared little for the pricing of short term bills, which should carry low interest rates, and longer term bonds. Their interest rates were more or less the same, at 2%. Eccles complained that this was distorting the market for bonds and preventing a proper yield curve for private banks holding of bonds, which for technical reasons affects banks' profitability. Plus ça change ...

8. The story is comprehensively related in Benn Steil, *The Battle for Bretton Woods*.

9. Although it is today the policy of the German government.

10. G. Magnifico and J. Williams, *European Monetary Integration*, Federal Trust Publication (1972), p.4.

11. *European Monetary Integration*, p. 4. This point is somewhat weakened on p. 6 where it is suggested that 'policy harmonisation should be primarily concentrated on monetary rather than fiscal instruments' – this, though, only being a feature of preliminary stages.

12. Angelos Delivorias *A History of European Monetary Integration* (European Parliamentary Research Service, March 2015; Members' Research Service PE 551.325).

13. See the epic chapter 'Shock Waves' on this unstable period by David Marsh, *The Euro: The Politics of a New Global Currency* (Yale University Press, 2009).

14. Marsh (*The Euro*, p. 132) records an illuminating quote from the French prime minister, Michel Rocard, who (in retrospect) observed: 'There was a balance between unification of Germany and the establishment of European monetary union. Both processes accelerated after the fall of the Berlin Wall. Kohl and Mitterrand were already engaged in both efforts.'

15. Harold James, *Making the European Monetary Union* (Harvard University Press, 2012), pp. 281-290.

16. The Bundesbank is statutorily independent of government (D. Marsh, *The Bundesbank*, London, Heinemann, 1992, p. 10). Its legal remit is to conduct monetary policy 'with the aim of safeguarding the currency'. This is its primary goal, but it is also required to support the economic policy of the Federal Government. See Stanley Fischer, 'Modern Central Banking' in *The Future of Central Banking*, ed. Capie, Goodhart, Fischer, Schnadt (Cambridge University Press, 1994), p. 264.

17. Stanley Fischer ('Modern Central Banking', p. 297) includes the complementary argument that centralised collective bargaining (the so-called Tariff agreement) 'is at least as much responsible for low inflation in Germany as is the independence of the Bundesbank'.

18. In 1992 the United Kingdom and Denmark had already given notification of their intention not to participate in the third stage of EMU and therefore not to adopt the euro. These two Member States therefore have an exemption with regard to their participation in EMU. The exemption arrangements are detailed in the protocols relating to these two countries annexed to the founding Treaties of the EU. However, the United Kingdom and Denmark reserve the option to end their exemption and submit applications to join the third phase of EMU. As things now stand, 19 of the 28 Member States have joined the third stage of EMU and thus have the euro as a single currency. However, Denmark does participate in ERMII, which has a special banding for Denmark of + or – 2.25% around the central rate of the Krone to Euro. This means that the independence of the Danish Central Bank is, thereby, limited in practice. Its aim is to keep the Krone within this narrow exchange rate band. However, the ECB is also obliged

to help protect the Danish currency in the case of speculative attacks. ERMII also operates, with the wider banding, to provide a pre-Eurozone space for EU countries wishing to adopt the Euro so as to ensure a high degree of exchange rate stability before formal entry into the Eurozone.

19. HPIC excluded housing costs, an essential component of living costs as well as asset price inflation.

20. This has recently been confirmed by Yanis Varoufakis, during his stormy sojourn on the Eurogroup as the Finance Minister for Greece. Varoufakis asked what was the constitutional position of Eurogroup (which was refusing emergency funding to Greece). A member of the Eurogroup's secretariat informs Varoufakis: 'Minister, the Eurogroup does not exist in law, as it not part of any of the EU treaties. It is an informal group of the finance ministers of the eurozone member states. Thus there are no written rules about the way it conducts its business, and therefore its president is not legally bound.' (*Adults in the Room*, Bodley Head, 2017, p. 447).

21. Quoted in Stanley Fischer 'Modern Central Banking', p. 265.

Chapter 3

Changes in the Roles of Central Banks

In this chapter we provide an overview of the recent approaches of central banks to their monetary policy delivery and the rationale behind the operational policies adopted. This overview covers the move to grant central banks independence, and its justification and implications; the shift from monetary aggregates targeting to inflation targeting; the move in approach and use of policy instruments following the GFC, and the CB claims for success in relation to economic recovery.

3.1 Recent CB Approaches

During the period of the 'Great Moderation' (c. 1995-2005), there was a remarkable convergence in the ways in which most OECD central banks went about their tasks – this despite the very many differences in the formal arrangements of those central banks within different nation states. The Great Moderation was a sustained period of growth, low inflation, and seemingly self-regulating markets. The commonly held economic doctrine (New Keynesianism and DSGE modeling) argued that state treasuries had to step back from macroeconomic steering of the economy, in particular to give up the policy of fiscally smoothing out the ups and downs in economic performance.

Under President Clinton's leadership, China entered the WTO leading to a transformation in the global economy. The leading economies allowed and supported the free flow of capital (though not China in this respect). Floating exchange rates and the existence of deep and supposedly stable bond markets meant that some of the previous tasks of central banks were becoming redundant. All economic agents, now freed up from the old restraints of national-economic regulation, were assumed to be rational in their market calculations and decisions. New Keynesians, in particular, stressed the notion of 'rational expectations'. Any government intervening too heavily in an economy would be anticipated, and market decisions would negate the intentions of policy makers. The problematic that defined economic doctrine in the 1980s and 1990s was price inflation, very much a feature of the disruptive 1970s. Working with the now discredited Phillips curve as a model[1], which held there was a direct tradeoff between inflation and unemployment, rational expectation theories argued that fiscal stimuli (to decrease unemployment) would be anticipated by all economic agents (both labour and capital) and the hoped for boost in growth would be dissipated through higher inflation.

This, then, was the mood music when the ECB was being designed in the late 1980s and 1990s and it also came to determine the way in which the Federal Reserve made its decisions. By the 1990s retail price inflation was no longer such a problem, giving central bankers a far easier time. Their favoured instrument was tweaking the rate of interest at which they lent to the banking sector, so keeping as they thought inflation within a narrow band around a nominal 2%. The underlying trend of inflation, anyway, was being pushed downwards with lowered global commodity prices (particularly oil) and the entrance of half a billion new Chinese workers into the world economy – amongst many other factors in play, including in some countries, e.g. the UK, a weakening of trade unions.

3.2 Central Bank Independence

On May 6 1997 the new British Government announced the operational independence of the Bank of England. Previously, the Bank's role in monetary policy had been advisory and the final decision on official interest rates remained with the Chancellor of the Exchequer. Under the new arrangements, the Bank of England was given full responsibility for setting monetary policy to achieve an inflation target. The previous intention to keep inflation below 2.5% was replaced by a point target of 2.5%. If inflation deviated from the target by more than 1 percentage point in either direction, the Bank's Governor was required to send an open letter to the Chancellor. This exercise repeated every three months as long as the deviation persisted.

The legislation of independence in many countries enabled central banks to take decisions on interest rates free from political interference. Prior to the grant of independence, central banks took their cues from the Treasury or Finance Ministry, which was an executive organ of an elected government. The most famous critic of central bank independence was Prime Minister Margaret Thatcher, who saw the derogation of this power to the Bank of England as a loss of monetary sovereignty. She refused to allow her Chancellor to go down this road.[2] In the United States the agreement of 1951 conceded the right of the Federal Reserve to decide on interest rate decisions.[3] In practice this 'independence' always remained a political issue. When an administration was running a budget deficit and/or reaching the limits of full economic capacity, the Federal Reserve's automatic response was to tighten interest rates and subdue credit expansion. By dint of long appointment periods, governors of the Federal Reserve could not be sacked and this ensured substantive autonomy. But disagreements between government and the Federal Reserve often became personalised battle of wills. Arthur Burns tried to stand up to President Nixon but was undermined by the dark arts of the Nixon White House.[4] President Bush Sr implored Paul Volcker not to be an inflation hawk prior to Bush's re-election, which he lost, for which he blamed Volcker. Volcker established the tradition of the Chair as a major personality, an image taken over by Alan Greenspan. Greenspan's pro-market stance, which presented few obstacles to credit expansion and financial innovation, caused no disagreement with the Bush Jr. White House. However the critics of the vast expansion of financial and banking power, in Congress, academia and publics, were effectively ignored by Chairman Greenspan, who spent considerable time on cultivating his image in the media and Washington circles.

Hence the principal criticism of central bank independence lies in the arrogation of directive financial influence without effective democratic check. From the perspective of institutional pluralism – very much a feature of federal constitutions – this meant that the decisions of one of the most important organs of executive power were beyond recall.

The ECB is in a different situation. Formally it is subordinate to the General Council of the European System of Central Banks. They, with the approval of the European Parliament, determine the ECB's mandate. Within that mandate, the ECB has operational autonomy, very much reinforced by the eight year-long appointments of the governors.[5] We have already noted the German insistence that the ECB be given operational independence; the intention here clearly was to ward off any accommodation of deficit budgets of (mainly) southern European nation-states. This introduces a regional note. There was no European Treasury, so a fortiori there could be no federal budget deficit. Instead deficits would be racked up by state governments, and this became the axis of conflict – of the ECB standing firm against those countries which broke the Maastricht budget rules. This regional dimension is explored in the next chapter. Here we just note the arguments for and against ECB independence.

The ECB's own position is encapsulated in a recent speech given in Frankfurt on March 30 2017 by Yves Mersch, Member of the Executive Board of the ECB. He acknowledges a number of academic studies which have been made on the topic of central bank independence, including recent ones, e.g. by Ed Balls, James Howat, and Anna Stansbury of the Harvard Kennedy School.[6]

Mersch provides four arguments in support of ECB independence: three are general arguments in favour and the fourth is sui generis to the ECB. We may take these arguments in turn. First, Mersch suggests that there is 'sound economic evidence' (though he cites no specific research) that 'price stability is conducive to economic growth and high levels of employment which, in turn, positively contribute to the welfare of citizens.'

One might agree with this as a general proposition, except that without some quantification it cannot be held to be self-evidently true. Mersch was making this case at a time when the ECB's own target rate had dropped, in June 2016, to minus .1%. On the contrary, there is 'sound economic evidence' that price deflation is very bad for growth and the economic welfare of citizens.

Insofar as inflation might rise above 2% would it also be acceptable for it to rise to 4%? Logically it would appear that a 4% variation may be acceptable to the ECB. Is there any level or rate of variation, particularly upward, which will threaten economic growth?

What we do know is that there was a consistent HICP rise from 2001 to 2013. At the same time economic growth rose until 2007 and then fell substantially during 2008 before slowly increasing in 2009 until falling again in 2011, and has been recovering over 2017. It therefore seems difficult to conclude on the evidence of the pattern of the evolution of prices and of economic growth, over this period, that there is any consistent relationship between variations in prices and variations in growth. This is not to suggest that substantial variations in inflation will not have any impact on growth. But it is more likely that any dislocation of growth will be caused by economic shocks which may or may not be accompanied by variations in inflation.

Second, Mersch suggests that 'in advanced economies central bank independence and inflation traditionally show a significant negative correlation', and that this has been shown by empirical studies. But Mersch is ambivalent here. He admits that in the studies – aside from instability of the post-breakdown of Bretton Woods and oil crisis period – the evidence appears to suggest that the correlation between political independence and inflation is unconvincing. Nonetheless, he still argues strongly in favour of political independence on the basis of the 'evidence'. He cites other literature, on rules versus discretion, which suggests that the political electoral cycle tends to create short-termism and inflationary pressures. However, he does also argue that 'independence does not mean isolation' – a useful phrase – and that democratic controls and accountability are required, if independence is to be sustained.

Third, Mersch argues that 'a clear and limited mandate is necessary for the parliament and the public to be able to monitor and evaluate the performance of the central bank'. Here he quotes Tinbergen who argued that institutions must not be overburdened with multiple goals without having the appropriate instruments to achieve them. This argument – implying a clear, limited operational mandate – is a strong one, irrespective of whether or not a central bank is independent. The ECB enjoys greater clarity than the Federal Reserve which has a multiple task mandate (Humphrey-Hawkins). In practice the discretionary power of the Federal Reserve Chair has interpreted this in favour of price stability.

Finally, Mersch makes a specific Eurozone/EU case for ECB independence by suggesting that: 'the euro area is not a nation state. Its institutional framework is shaped by the fact that a single European monetary policy co-exists with national or shared sovereignty in various policy domains. Fiscal and labour market policies are particularly relevant in this regard'. Hence, Mersch goes on to argue: 'In such an environment, it is important to have an independent institution which provides the various national decision-makers within the monetary union with a stable nominal anchor enshrined in Union primary law'.

This goes to the nub of why the ECB is different. Unlike other central banks the ECB is operating in a confederal system. This distinction, clear in theory, has complex practical implications when the performance of the ECB and the Fed are compared (in Chapter 4 below). In this regard Mersch emphasizes the institutional distinctiveness of the EZ arrangements. Institutional independence refers to the prohibition of the influence of third parties -e.g. national politicians- on the structure, functioning, decision-making, and exercise of powers of the central bank. As a consequence, the ECB is insulated from claims and demands generated for whatever reasons from individual nation-states or groupings of the same. Once the door is closed for a meeting of the ECB governing board, they have no rule-based obligation to heed the special pleading of any one finance minister, whether from Germany or Greece. To this end the ECB has instrumental independence. This means it can determine its policy tools in pursuit of price stability without interference. It has legal discretion to use and clarify its own monetary policy instruments such as outright purchases, the collateral framework and its counterparties.

At a personal level governors cannot be removed during their eight year terms, and this is laid down in Treaty. On financial independence Mersch suggests that Financial independence is so important that it is explicitly listed in Article 282(3) of the Treaty, which provides that the ECB is independent with regard to the management of its finances, meaning budgetary autonomy and ensuring that the ECB has sufficient capital, staff and income to perform independently the tasks conferred on it by the Treaty and the Statute of the ESCB. In addition, Article 14.4 of the Statute of the ESCB provides the Governing Council with a veto power to object to national functions/actions of National Central Banks (NCBs) that interfere with the objectives and tasks of the ESCB, thus further safeguarding, among other things, central bank financial independence. The NCBs cannot assume tasks that would endanger their ability, from a financial perspective, to carry out ESCB-related tasks.

All these measures buttress and guarantee the institutional insulation of the ECB. In a sense, these measures are an essential feature of a central bank operating in a confederal political system. In a federal political system, state particularity has already been resolved (through the institutions of Congress, and the Senate; and of course both of these had a democratically deliberative role in the creation and any alteration of the Federal Reserve). There is nothing *faux* about the independence of the ECB. Whether it may be better to be a nation of laws rather than a community of laws in this respect, we leave as an open question for the moment.

3.3 Shifting from Monetary Aggregates to Inflation Targeting (Converging Mandates)

In outlining the remit of the European Central Bank and the Federal Reserve System this section draws on the official literature, the Bank of International Settlements (BIS) in particular. The intention is to outline the common characteristics between the monetary policies in Europe and the United States that led to the similarities of the mandates of the ECB and the Federal Reserve. In fact, the growing similarities in central banks' remit in 1980s and 1990s can be observed in all advanced countries (including Japan, Australia, New Zealand and Canada).[7]

In late 1990s (1997/98), the ECB adopted a system of combining elements of monetary targeting and explicit inflation targeting. Although these targeting strategies differ, in practice any differences were small. First, it was intended that the ECB would publicly define what it understood by price stability. In the light of its mandate, this definition would influence the inflation expectations of economic units. Secondly, monetary aggregates used as information variables at that time were also used in countries with explicit inflation targets. In the past, central banks that employed monetary targets had relied upon them to guide policy in the medium term while still allowing the near-term inflation outlook to play an important role in defining the interest rates.

Monetary targeting requires a firm understanding of the money demand (MD) to set target ranges and to determine what policy measures are necessary to achieve the targets. Thus it was difficult to control the aggregates after the establishment of the European Monetary Union (EMU) due to considerable structural changes expected to take place in the member-states. Essentially, the monetary transmission mechanisms of the Eurozone (EZ) were unknown and changing given the expansion of the EZ with new countries joining (in 2017, 19 from the initial 11)

Inflationary targeting requires the construction of an inflation forecast in order to determine the path for short-term interest rates that is required to reach the targets. The inflation process within the EZ was expected to change in an unpredictable way after the introduction of the euro, which made it difficult initially for the ECB to conduct monetary policy by using only inflation targeting, though it subsequently moved to inflation targeting alone.

In most countries with inflation targets (the US, in Europe, and in Japan), the main challenge for monetary policy had been to promote monetary conditions that preserve the good inflation performance through the economic upswing, thereby helping to make the economic expansion a long-lasting one. To the end of 1990s, initially low policy rates needed to be raised, although the timing of the policy tightening differed across countries depending on the initial conditions and the effects of the Asian crisis.

Table 3.1: Policy Rates and Starting Dates of the sample period

Country	Policy rate	Starting date
Australia	Official target rate	23/01/1990
Austria	GOMEX	6/05/1985
Belgium	Central rate	29/01/1991
Canada	Operating band	15/04/1994
France	Tender rate	4/01/1982
Germany	Repurchase rate	19/06/1979
Spain	Repurchase rate	14/05/1990
Sweden	Repurchase rate	1/06/1994
United States	Federal funds target rate	10/08/1989

Source: BIS, 68th Annual Report, Table IV.1, p. 68; 1998

Overall the move towards higher transparency in the CBs actions was observed in the 1990s, as a result the inflation targeting regimes were established. The transparency pertained not only to the central bank's objectives, but also to its operational framework (instruments and procedures employed). This move towards greater clarity of the objective of price stability was most obvious in the countries with explicit inflation targets, but could be observed in other countries too.

The European Monetary Institute had agreed that the ECB would provide a public definition of its final objective of price stability. When it came to it there was considerable discussion within the EP on the specific numerical inflation target, within the overall price stability objective for the ECB. Ultimately the target was fixed as 'an inflation rate in the Eurozone area of below, but close to, 2% over the medium term', as measured by the HCIP (Harmonised Index of Consumer Prices).

One exception remained the United States, where various congressional proposals to clarify the Federal Reserve's mandate at that time failed to be translated into new legislation. As described by Sebastian Mallaby in his biography of Alan Greenspan, the Federal Open Market Committee somewhat accidentally alighted on its 2% target in 1998. Retail price inflation by that date was well under control due to factors in the world economy. Hence in the light of a convincing rationale for the role of the FOMC, the inflation target offered a formal benchmark of a not too punishing nature.[8]

Table 3.2: Monetary Policy Transparency

Targets	US	Japan[9]	DE[10]	Canada	UK	Sweden	Austria
Objectives							
Price stability	N	N/Y	Y	Y	Y	Y	Y
Quantified objective	N	N/N	Y	Y	Y	Y	Y
Strategy							
Inflation reports	N	N/Y	Y	Y	Y	Y	Y
Regular Parliament hearings	Y	Y/Y	N	Y	Y	Y	Y
Intermediate targets[11]	N	N/N	Y	N	Y	Y	N
Operational procedures							
Announcement of policy decisions	Y	N/Y	Y	Y	Y	Y	Y
Announcement of desired future path	N	N/N	N	N	N	N	N
Publication of minutes[12]	Y	N/Y	N	N	Y	N	N

Source: BIS, 68th Annual Report, Table IV.2, p. 70; 1998

Since the early 1990s, central banks in most of the English-speaking countries began to announce changes in their operating targets too. The US changes in the federal funds target rate have since February 1994 been announced on the day of the Federal Open Markets Committee (FOMC) meeting. The goal was to eliminate any ambiguity about the stance of policy. Also, the necessity of having to explain to the public the reasons for policy changes had some of the advantages such as greater rigour in the central bank's internal debates and decisions; a clearer focus on the objectives and a greater public acceptance of monetary policy decisions.

There was an increasing tendency to forewarn markets regularly about possible future policy moves through speeches and other publications; so-called 'forward guidance'. For example, Chairman Greenspan of the FED signaled the 1994 interest rate tightening in his Humphrey-Hawkins testimony in the autumn of 1993. It was commonly agreed that at a strategic level the transparency was desirable. The requirements laid down in the Maastricht Treaty for the ECB to publish quarterly reports and present an annual report to the European Parliament were equally significant measures in order to establish the ECB's reputation.

Transparency, forward guidance, explicit targeting, and reporting back to the legislature was the new modus operandi of central banking. The economy and the markets could be talked to and they would respond. At least that was the theory. In practice, it is not clear how much of the forward guidance is already discounted by the markets. However, in a sense this does not matter, it simply means that the central bank is another, albeit important, market participant, and its statement are not *'ex cathedra'* pronouncements.

3.4 New Basis of Monetary Policy

Given the exclusive focus on interest rates, it is worth evaluating the economic theory that currently underpins central bankers practice. Sir Charles Bean, a recently retired Deputy Governor of the Bank of England has given us this statement of the doctrine:

'The past couple of decades have witnessed a remorseless fall in the real rate of interest consistent with macroeconomic equilibrium — the "natural" rate. The causes are still a matter of debate. Some point to higher savings, others to the impact of slow productivity growth on investment. Balance-sheet repair has surely been important, too.

While central banks can set any policy rate they want in the short run, if they are to achieve their objectives over the long term it must converge to the sum of the natural rate and their target inflation rate. Criticism from politicians that central banks' policies are penalising savers and driving up asset prices misses the point: the decline in interest rates ultimately reflects forces that central bankers are powerless to change.'[13]

Needless to say the current low rate of interest is a matter of considerable controversy, as is the theory of the 'natural' rate of interest which is used by central bankers to justify their policies and actions. Mario Draghi, President of the ECB, mounts the same defence, arguing that the natural rate of interest is itself very low and is ultimately driving interest rates down near to zero.[14] So to ensure that interest rates return to higher levels, thereby raising the natural rate, Draghi has stated that this requires a focus on policies which can address the root causes of excess saving over investment; in other words, fiscal and structural policies and, in particular, raising investment demand and productivity (based on structural reforms).

This stance, as Draghi indicates below, is one which entails acceptance of the New Keynesian ('Wicksellian') argument that:

'The natural rate of interest – which is the real interest rate that balances desired saving and planned investment, at a level consistent with output being at potential and stable prices – has fallen over time, to very low or even negative levels. And whatever the drivers behind this, central banks have to take it into account and cut their policy rates to commensurately lower levels.

Indeed, the way standard monetary policy works is to steer real short-term interest rates so that they "shadow" the natural rate, which keeps the economy in balance and prices stable. When inflation is below our objective and there is a negative output gap, monetary policy has to bring real rates below the natural rate to provide enough demand support. And when inflation is above our objective and the output gap is positive, the reverse is true.

If central banks did not act in this way – that is, if they did not lower short-term rates in tandem with the natural rate – market rates would be too high relative to the real returns in the economy, and investing would become unattractive. The economy would therefore be pushed away from full capacity and price stability. By contrast, by holding market rates below the real rate of return, we encourage the investment and consumption that is needed to bring the economy back to potential.'

This position, it should be noted, is a pre-Keynesian theoretical position which has been smuggled back into New-Keynesian theory, for example by Woodford.[15] It postulates that savings and investment are brought into equilibrium by the 'natural/neutral' rate of interest (*despite the fact that this rate is unobservable*). It is important to appreciate how this now conventional central bankers' position came to be. It followed the 1990s abandonment of the Friedmanite monetary aggregate approach, which had proved unworkable (despite the ECB's early affection for monetary aggregates as control variables).

In July 1993 Alan Greenspan told the Congress that:

'In assessing real rates, the central issue is their relationship to an equilibrium interest rate, specifically the real rate level that, if maintained, would keep the economy at its production potential over time. Rates persisting above that level, history tells us, tend to be associated with ... disinflation ... and rates below that level tend to be associated with eventual resource bottlenecks and rising inflation, which ultimately engender economic contraction.'[16]

Greenspan's 'equilibrium interest rate' is the equivalent of Knut Wicksell's earlier 'natural interest rate' theory which was dominant in the days before the Great Depression and before its demolition by Keynes in his *General Theory*.

So essentially, as Draghi demonstrates, the argument is that if prices are rising then the interest rate must be below the natural/neutral rate and vice versa. So, without being able to observe the natural rate we can tell where real interest rates are, i.e. either below or above, purely determined by observing whether commodity prices are rising or falling.

In this manner, it is held, monetary policy is able to influence, *to a degree*, aggregate demand, particularly if accompanied by structural (i.e. labour market) reform; exactly as described by Draghi.

3.5 Changing Operational Tools after the GFC

When the global financial crisis broke, finally, in 2008, the central bankers were stunned. Lender of last resort belonged to the rule book of another age (Bagehot's *Lombard Street*, 1873). Central bankers had almost no instruments to bring the situation under some sort of control. They could drop their target rate, which they did reluctantly in a number of steps. But in a crisis the problem is not the price of debt, it is the availability of debt paper that can be transacted. Banks and money markets no longer placed any faith in the viability of counterparties who they otherwise in normal times would have trusted. Bagehot prescribed buying all sound debt paper from approved financial institutions and in a bank run panic virtually any paper. This is akin to a massive open market operation. Because the central bank can emit (aka print) any amount of currency, it is able to inject cash (liquidity) back into the seized up financial system. Central banks will seek indemnification for this from their government Treasury, though usually this remains a secret or tacit agreement. It is the Treasury, and behind it citizen taxation, that ultimately is the guarantor of last resort.

However, it should be noted that the substantial intervention of central banks, in buying risky assets against higher risk assets (credit easing), and eventually buying vast amounts of sovereign debt (quantitative easing), was required, not simply to provide liquidity, but to allow banks and other financial institutions to repair their balance sheets. The GFC was a balance sheet crisis with a number of large institutions becoming insolvent on balance sheets. In some cases financial institutions were allowed to 'go to the wall', most notably Lehman Bros in the US; in the UK, RBS and Northern Rock were taken over by the state, and, effectively, AIG in the US; or forced into mergers, HBOS in the UK, and Bears Sterns in the US.

These interventions, by both the state and subsequently by the central banks represented a new and substantial expansion of the normal open market operations used to maintain the target rates of interest, e.g. the federal funds rate. So much so that the new nomenclature of credit easing (CE) and quantitative easing (QE) was used to distinguish the new era of massive central bank interventions.

The other important point to note is that governments themselves were constrained by central bank independence. Demand management policy had been entrusted to monetary measures alone. Governments no longer had the confidence to embark directly with infrastructure expenditure – renewing schools, renewing roads and infrastructure, investing in human capital and science – which otherwise would have lifted economies out of financially-induced recession.[17] 'Unconventional' also signified this loss of fiscal steering capacity, placing an impossible burden and unrealizable expectations on monetary measures alone.

The analysis demonstrates the pivotal position of central banks in providing ample liquidity and recapitalising funds to restore financial markets functioning during crises, via huge interventions. They can suppress long-term interest rates through large-size purchases of bonds. Gagnon (2016) estimates the median effect on the yield curve to be a 20 basis points (a fifth of one percent) reduction for a bonds purchase equal to 10% of Japanese GDP.[18] This is somewhat lower in comparison to the median reduction effects in the US, UK and the Eurozone, where the median is about 45-55 basis points, but understandably the Japanese Government Bonds market is relatively larger to the GDP in Japan, and thus, requires more persistent and targeted actions.

In fact, the central banks can lower the entire yield curve, which is what the Bank of Japan has been exercising since September 2016. Simultaneously, they influence the short-term interest rates via their policy rate targets and reduce the real interest rates, which pushes up the inflationary expectations.

How successful these new and unprecedented CB interventions have been, not only in resolving the problems of a fractured financial sector, but also in attempting to restore economic growth, we will consider in the next chapter.

Federal Central Banks

Notes

1. See James Forder, *Macroeconomics and the Phillips Curve Myth* (Oxford University Press, 2014).
2. In 1990 Mrs Thatcher interviewed in the Wall Street Journal said that in the British system it is government that sets monetary policy and this 'is the essence of democratic control. There is no way we would give it up, nor is it necessary to give it up.' Quote by W. Keegan, *The Observer* 28 January 1990.
3. Allan Meltzer, *History of Federal Reserve*, vol 1, p. 711.
4. Sebastian Mallaby, *The Man Who Knew. The Life and Times of Alan Greenspan* (London, NY: Bloomsbury, 2016), pp. 140-144,
5. Following Stanley Fischer, this division of mandates and operational autonomy, is termed goal independence and instrument independence ('Modern Central Banking', in Capie et al, *Future of Central Banking*, p. 292.)
6. Ed Balls, James Howat, Anna Stansbury, 'Central Bank Regulation Revisited: After the financial crisis, what should a model central bank look like?', M-RCBG Associate Working Paper No. 67, 2016.
7. BIS, 68th Annual Report, 1998
8. Sebastian Mallaby, *The Man Who Knew. The Life and Times of Alan Greenspan* (London, NY: Bloomsbury, 2016), p. 488. Prior to 1998 Janet Yellen had argued against adoption of an inflation target.
9. The second entry in the column refers to the new Bank of Japan Law from April 1998
10. DE = Germany; N= No; Y= Yes
11. M3 growth target in Germany; published inflation forecasts in Sweden and the UK
12. The publication lag in the US and UK is about 6 weeks
13. Charles Bean, 'Central banking has never looked so daunting', FT, 3 December, 2017.
14. Mario Draghi, Speech in Berlin, October 2016.
15. M. Woodford *Interest and Prices. Foundations of a Theory of Monetary Policy* (Princeton: Princeton University Press, 2003).
16. Alan Greenspan, 'Statement to Congress', *Federal Reserve Bulletin* (Sept 1993), pp. 849-855.

17. Where they did have such confidence, as in Australia under PM Kevin Rudd, the economy greatly improved and more quickly.

18. Gagnon J., 'Quantitative Easing: An underappreciated success', PB16-4, The Peterson Institute of International Economics, 2016.

Chapter 4

Assessing the Effectiveness of Central Bank Responses to the Global Financial Crisis

4.1 General

This chapter compares the reactions of the monetary authorities in the US and the EU to the global financial crisis (GFC) and sets out the empirical data. The GFC impacts had not the same timing in relation to the EZ and the US, and because of the differing monetary transmission systems and the more limited freedom of action of the ECB, care has to be taken in assessing the effectiveness across the two different economic spaces. Our analysis shows that the coordinated intervention strategies of the US Treasury with the Federal Reserve were more effective and more varied than those undertaken in Europe. The margin of difference in outcomes is not large when measured by macroeconomic indicators such as percentage growth in GDP, and retail price inflation – reaching 2% being the challenge on the latter. Unemployment, however, was far worse in Europe. What was common to both countries was the extraordinary extent of monetary intervention, historically without precedent, in order to restore some functioning normality to the banking and financial system. And again common to both economies, was the disappointing revival in the real economy of jobs, wages, consumption and investment. When the economic welfare foregone is estimated then the case for monetary only solutions has to be questioned. We leave the political consequences of this loss of economic welfare to Chapter 6, other than to note that the far more complex political structures of the European Union exacted a higher price of the Union itself.

4.2 Tracking the Unconventional Operational Measures Used

The intent of this section is to explain and track the unconventional measures that the Federal Reserve System in the US and the European Central Bank in Europe had to take in order to support the financial sector during the Global Financial Crisis. It will be presented as a comparative case and also in some detail because the full extent of these measures is only rarely laid out openly.

If one focuses on the US and EU monetary easing, one can notice that while the Fed began instantly with the large-scale asset purchases in November 2008, the ECB applied a more gradual approach with smaller amounts of purchases initially and it was not until 2013/14 that quantitative easing began in earnest. The Fed continued with the **Large-S**cale **A**sset

Purchases from 2008 and ran it over in three stages as
LSAP1, LSAP2 and LSAP3 until early 2014 (see Table 4.1),
while the ECB is still progressing with the non-standard
measures into 2018 (see Table 4.2).

4.3 The FED non-standard monetary measures

**Table 4.1: The Federal Reserve's large-scale
asset purchase (LSAP) programme**

	Announcement	Termination	Assets-purchased	Amounts
LSAP1	Nov 2008		Agency mortgage-backed securities (MBS) and agency debt	$600 billion
	March 2009		Agency securities	$850 billion
		March 2010	Longer-term US Treasury securities	$300 billion
LSAP2	Nov 2010	June 2011	Longer-term US Treasury securities	$600 billion
Maturity Extension Programme (MEP)	September 2011		US Treasury securities with remaining maturities of 6 to 30 years	$400 billion
	June 2012	Dec 2012	US Treasury securities with remaining maturities of 6 to 30 years	
LSAP3	September 2012	Oct 2014	Agency MBS	$40 billion per month
	Dec 2012	Oct 2014	Longer-term US Treasury securities	$45 billion per month[1]

Source: US Federal Reserve website

In reading Table 4.1 we should be aware of the important
distinction between *quantitative easing* and *credit easing*. In
contrast to quantitative easing (QE), which increases the size
of the central bank's balance sheet, credit easing (CE) shifts

the composition of the balance sheet away from default-free assets and toward assets with credit risk where the borrower can default. In the absence of private demand for the risky asset, the central bank's purchases make credit available where no alternative existed. Under QE risk free treasury bonds are bought, bringing down the general interest rate structure. When the Federal Reserve Banks purchase assets with risk of default and uncertain re-sale value, predominantly mortgage backed securities (MBS), CE will tend to narrow the interest rate spread of MBS over Treasuries, making it less costly to obtain a mortgage. Table One under the column 'Assets-purchased' reveals the mix of both QE and CE at certain points of time.

The Federal Reserve's shift to CE in the financial crisis has been virtually unprecedented in scale. Chart 4.1 provides a clearer picture on the evolution of the credit risk assets that the Fed holds. While the grey-shaded portions of the chart do not involve default risk, the portions shaded in other colours typically do. The chart shows that assets with default risk now predominate for the first time.

**Chart 4.1: United States – Composition of Fed Assets
(Millions of U.S. Dollars), Jan 07-Jun 09.**

Billions of dollars

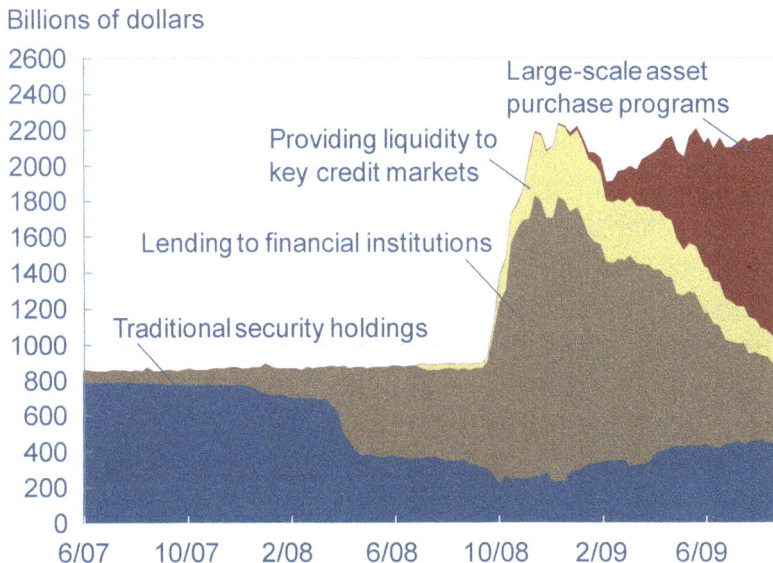

Source: Federal Reserve Bank of Cleveland.

The impact of various Fed CE interventions has been significant. One early example is the Fed's Commercial Paper Funding Facility (CPFF), which purchases three month CP directly from borrowers (these purchases make up the largest portion of 'liquidity to key credit markets' in Chart 4.1). When private CP lending collapsed temporarily during the crisis, the CPFF made credit available to high-quality borrowers who otherwise might have been unable to finance their inventories and payrolls. As conditions in the CP market improved, the need for Fed intervention declined and its CP holdings peaked early in 2009.

Aside from direct lending to financial institutions, the largest example of Fed CE during the crisis is the acquisition of mortgage backed securities (MBS). The early 2009 announcement of the Fed's MBS plans already helped narrow MBS interest rate spreads and lower mortgage yields. As of mid-2009, the Fed had purchased more than $425 billions of MBS. As a result, the volume of MBS surpassed that of traditional securities on the Fed's balance sheet (see Chart 4.1). And the Fed offered to purchase a sizable additional volume of MBS in the remainder of 2009.

Although both central banks undertook different means of monetary easing, and the large-scale purchases of sovereign and private assets are considered by some as a more effective means of easing, the effects on national economies and international markets seem to be not that dissimilar as the evidence below will demonstrate.

However, the Fed was the first to begin with the reduction of the asset purchases to $10 billion in January 2014, and as the US economy's recovery improved, they decided to end it in October 2014. The overall size of its asset holdings has been maintained through the reinvestment of principal payments in agency mortgage-backed securities.

As a result of these unconventional measures, the balance sheet and the asset holdings of the Fed have experienced an unprecedented expansion since the second half of 2008, and reached the level of nearly $4.5 trillion in 2015 (see Table 4.5, addendum). It kept the same amount of asset holdings in 2016 and most of 2017. It was proposed back in September 2014 that the reduction in initial stages would be accomplished passively and predictably, and not before the normalisation of interest rates, by allowing debt to run off when it matures with no active asset sales in the bond markets. This implied a gradual and steady reduction of balance sheet's asset holdings with minimal shocks to the markets, which means that the Fed will be decreasing their activities over a period of about 10 years

as suggested by the still open debate on this topic[2]. The Federal
Reserve officials project to reduce their balance sheet from 23%
of GDP to 10% of GDP over a period of 8 years (until 2025).

In September 2017 Janet Yellen announced the Federal
Reserve would actually start reversing its asset buying
programme. A $4.5 trillion portfolio produces a multi-billion
income stream to the Fed. In small steps this income would
not be used to buy more assets, to replace existing bonds as
they matured. In this way the Fed's balance sheet would gradually be reduced. An 8 year time scale suggests a withdrawal
of spending by the Fed of $500 billion a year – a reminder that
central banks are still in the realm of the unconventional.[3]

Table 4.5 (see addendum to this chapter) presents the
combined financial statements of the whole Federal Reserve
System for 2015 and 2016. It demonstrates the unavoidable
increase in asset holdings by the central bank system due to
expanded purchases of Treasury securities and government-
sponsored enterprise mortgage-backed securities. On the
liability side, one can see the large increase of deposits and
reserves sitting at the Federal Reserve, which combined
together account for about 70% of the assets' value. This
is partially a result of the more constrained capital environment and stricter bank regulations.

Unconventional monetary policy in regard to the heavy
engineering of driving bond yields down has had a very detri-
mental effect on the availability of reliable collateral. Large
commercial banks under new regulations require this, preferably T bonds, as do insurance companies. But the Federal
Reserve Banks have been buying up prime and not so prime
collateral. This collateral ensures the efficient functioning
of financial markets and shortage of collateral could deteri-
orate the functioning of financial systems.[4] In the combined
financial statement of Fed (see Table 4.5), the value of US

treasuries is \$2.5 trillion in 2016, which accounts for 55% of the total assets of the Fed. Other recent literature has focused on how the increased reliance on collateral may pose financial stability risks. For instance, Infante (2014)[5] uses a theoretical model to show that dealers that act as intermediaries in the market can be exposed to the risk of a sharp withdrawal of funding by collateral providers.

4.4 The ECB non-standard monetary measures

The ECB undertook a more gradual path of monetary easing in comparison to the FED and it intervened in October 2008 with 'enhanced credit support', directly providing liquidity to banks through fixed-rate instead of variable rate tenders, with full allotment. The ECB extended the list of eligible collaterals later, adjusting the quality thresholds for particular asset classes. Table 4.2 provides comprehensive information about all schemes ran by the ECB from October 2008 until now.

The European System of Central Banks, via the ECB, provided liquidity in foreign currencies against Euro denominated collateral, using reciprocal currency swaps with the Federal Reserve, the Bank of England, the Swiss National Bank, and the Bank of Japan. In May 2009, the ECB announced its first **C**overed **B**ond **P**urchase **P**rogramme (CBPP1) of EUR 60 billion. It was implemented between July 2009 and June 2010. The intention was to support 'a specific financial market segment that is important for the funding of banks and that had been particularly affected by the financial crisis'. The CBPP2 was implemented between November 2011 and October 2012, and it reached EUR 16.4 billion. Consequently, CBPP3 began in 2014 for two years and the bond purchase reached EUR 131 billion.

Table 4.2: The European Central Bank's non-standard monetary measures

	Start	Termination	Programme	Amount
LTRO1	Oct 2008	March 2009	Enhanced **L**onger-**T**erm **R**efinancing **O**perations, 3 and 6-months; fixed-rate full allotment	EUR 300 billion
	June 2009	December 2009	12-month fixed rate allotment	EUR 442 billion
CBPP1	July 2009	June 2010	**C**overed **B**ond **P**urchase **P**rogramme	EUR 60 billion
SMP	May 2010	September 2012	**S**ecurities **M**arkets **P**rogramme, sterilised	>EUR 200 billion
CBPP2	Nov 2011	Oct 2012	Covered bond purchase programme	EUR 16.4 billion
LTRO2	Oct &Dec 2011, Dec 2011, Feb 2012		12- &13-month LTROs; Three-year fixed-rate full-allotment	EUR 529 billion
OMT	September 2012		**O**utright **M**onetary **T**ransactions, government bonds of one to three years	Open-ended[6]
TLTRO-I	Sept 2014	June 2016	**T**argeted **L**onger-term **R**efinancing **O**perations	
EAPP		Sept 2016	**E**xpanded **A**sset **P**urchase **P**rogramme	EUR 60 billion per month
CBPP3	Oct 2014	At least 2 years	Covered bond purchase programme	EUR 131.14 billion
ABSPP	Nov 2014	At least 2 years	Longer-term US Treasury securities	EUR 14.58 billion
PSPP	March 2015	Sept 2016	**P**ublic **S**ector **P**urchase **P**rogramme	EUR 393,64 billion
EAPP	Sept 2016	March 2017	Expanded asset purchase programme	EUR 80 billion per month
TLTRO-II	March 2016	Dec 2016	Targeted longer-term refinancing operations	
EAPP	April 2017	Dec 2017 – open ended	Asset purchase programme	EUR 60 billion per month

Source: European Central Bank website

In June 2014, the ECB announced a series of targeted long-term refinancing operations that were conducted between 2014 and 2016, all maturing in September 2018. The targeted operations were carried out to improve bank lending to the euro area non-financial private sector. In January 2015, the ECB was fighting with the low inflation, and therefore announced an **E**xpanded **A**sset **P**urchase **P**rogramme (EAPP), which added the public-sector purchase programme to the other two programmes – CBPP3 and ABSPP. The public sector purchases took place between March 2015 and September 2016, which allowed the ECB to purchase bonds issued by euro area central, regional and local governments, agencies, international organisations and multilateral development banks located in the Euro area. The EAPP was implemented at a rate of EUR 60 billion per month, then the amount was increased to EUR 80 billion, and from April 2017 it was reduced again back to EUR 60 billion until inflation is consistent with the 'below, but close to 2%' target over the medium-term. It will be further reduced to EUR 30 billion per month from January 2018. Also in the context of its forward guidance, the ECB has expressed the readiness to increase the asset purchases in terms of size or duration, if a less favourable outlook in financial conditions were to materialise.

The institutional rationality of the ECB buying the bonds of its participant member states appears to be 'incestuous', or at least an interesting internal loop. The move, while wholly defensible in preventing further deflation in the EZ, highlights *the inability of the ECB to issue its own bonds*, which could then be repurchased in the event of a necessitating crisis. At the same time pressure from the EZ Eurogroup austerity policy position prevented individual member state governments from pursuing active fiscal policies to reflate their economies. The arguments for and against these moves, which were also highly political, goes to heart of federal and confederal institutional design of the EZ. This is discussed in chapters 6 and 7.

The non-standard measures have supported inflationary expectations and also have had an impact on the ECB's intention to keep short-term interest rates low for some time. The average amount of liquidity provided through open market operations – both tender operations and the asset purchases – increased by EUR 257.2 billion over the second half of 2016 to reach EUR 2,179.90 billion at the beginning of 2017 (see Table 4.6, addendum). The increase came primarily from the expanded asset purchase programme. Through the public sector purchase programme, the average liquidity increased by EUR 227.40 billion to reach EUR 1,616.70. As a consequence, the average excess liquidity rose by EUR 172 billion to stand at EUR 1,186.70 billion at the end of January. This was mainly reflected in higher average current account holdings of about EUR 867.80 billion[7].

Table 4.6 in the Addendum to this chapter presents the liquidity status of the whole Eurosystem from July 2016 until January 2017, and the figures discussed can be compared with Table 4.5 in the addendum.

4.5 Economic Assessment of Measures Taken

This is a subject that has yet to receive full objective, scientific assessment. The sheer scale of these measures – and their continuation over such a long period, bearing in mind it took Roosevelt four years to turn the US economy around (1933-37), make immediate assessment difficult. Many of the assessment studies have been conducted by institutions heavily involved in their implementation. Market indicators do not adequately register the need for the socio-economic alleviation of differentially distressed economies.

That noted, the IMF as a major institution engaged with finding solutions to the global financial crisis, commented that such monetary policies successfully restored market functioning and intermediation in the early phase of the GFC, but their continuation carried risks. Fratzscher et al (2013) find that earlier limited US QE measures were highly effective in lowering the sovereign yields and supporting equity prices. However, after 2010 such measures had indistinct effects on the yields across countries.[8] They also discussed in a different paper that ECB non-standard measures had beneficial impact on euro area asset prices and reduced bond market fragmentation, with positive cross-border impact on global equity markets.[9]

In addition, Chen, Lombardi, Ross and Zhu in a BIS Working Paper estimated that the US QE generally had stronger domestic and cross-border effects than the ECB non-standard measures.[10] In terms of the US economy, the authors demonstrate the US QE has had a larger impact on the real GDP growth and inflation (with more persistent increases) than euro area output and inflation responses. The macroeconomic data appears to support this conclusion, but in the absence of a full macro-economic assessment, taking into account fiscal measures and other relevant economic causal factors these studies cannot be said to be conclusive.

As for the impact on credit, the effects were broadly similar and statistically significant in the US and Europe. They argue that the domestic credit channels do work well for the unconventional monetary policy, but the transmission is rather weak, and this does raise the question of how reliable the monetary policy's transmission mechanism is. And the third conclusion the authors have made, suggests that the

US QE is much more effective in boosting investor confidence and supporting equity prices, but without recognising that some of this investment was directed into much riskier assets. In contrast, the euro area non-standard measures have had little impact on its equity prices, which is in part related to the more constrained role of the equities in Europe and a more active use of loan funding of business. Overall, Chen et al (2017) concluded that the domestic effects tend to be larger and more significant in the US economy as a result of better confidence and credit channelling.

The estimation made by Joseph Gagnon from the Peterson Institute for International Economics claims that the cumulative effects of the Fed QE rounds represented a 2.5% percentage point cut in the federal funds rate. Plus, the unemployment was reduced by more than 1% percentage point as of early 2015, and the inflation was boosted by nearly half a percentage point[11]. Similarly, the ECB President Mario Draghi announced at a 2015 Banking Congress an estimate that the equivalent reduction in lending rates following the launch of QE in the euro area (since 2008) was comparable to what would be expected from a 1% percentage point cut in the policy interest rate.[12]

However, though these impacts clearly benefitted the financial sector the overall economic impact should be regarded as more tenuous and less certain, despite the CB claims.

The variation in the application of the measures between the EZ and the US is also relevant here. Chart 4.2 below indicates a view of the central bank balance sheets of both the Fed and the ECB, together with those of the Bank of Japan and the Bank of England for comparison.

Chart 4.2: Central banks' balance-sheets. January 2007 = 100

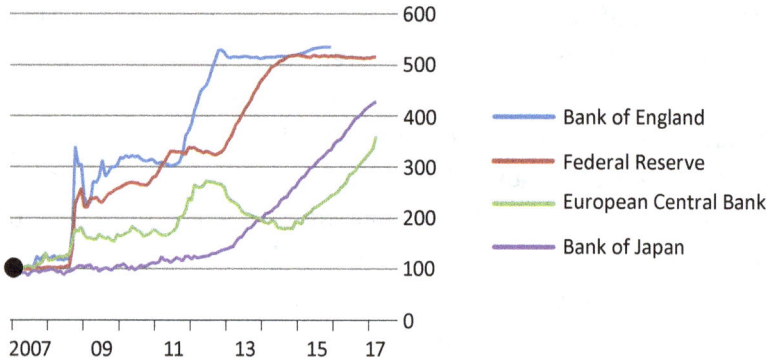

Source: National statistics, Haver Analytics

This indicates the wavering response of the ECB to the GFC. Chart 4.2 plots the extent to which various CBs pursued unorthodox monetary policy involving Quantitative Easing (QE). Both the Fed and the Bank of England (BoE) were quickest off the mark, in part because financial circumstances in both countries were the most severe, involving as they did, a meltdown in the residential property market. From 2007 to 2008, the Fed and the BoE tripled the assets on their balance sheets as they embarked on aggressive QE policies. The BoE, followed by the Fed then increased assets to 5 times their initial level between 2012 and 2013. These values have only marginally come down since then.

The response of the ECB was more modest, in part because of underlying internal tensions within the Eurozone about what the extent of QE should be. The ECB balance sheet nearly doubled in size between 2007 and 2011. Asset growth rose to around 250% of 2007 values in 2012/13 as the sovereign debt crisis hit. There was then a fall in assets owned to 2015, as QE programmes were reined back in again.

This was then followed in 2016 and 2017 by a belated and steep rise in ECB assets to around 3 ½ times their starting values. This may go some way to contributing to the weak economic recovery following the GFC. And responsibility for this rests, in large part, with the ECB. While Draghi said that he 'would do what it takes' to save the Eurozone, Chart 4.2 suggests that, in fact, this is not what happened.

4.6 Bailouts

The formation of the troika bail-out of Greece will be discussed in Chapter 6. It is the most controversial of the bailout packages. It politicised to an unacceptable extent the rescue of smaller economies, as in the case of Spain, Portugal as well as Greece. Five Euro-zone countries requested bailouts at various times and for differing reasons applicable to the specific experiences of the individual countries' situations. The table below indicates the nature of the measures applied at EZ level: to Greece, Ireland, Portugal, Spain and Cyprus.

Federal Central Banks

Table 4.3: European bail-outs

Date	Country	Loan – type	EU/ECB	IMF	Reasons	Conditionality
21 April 2010	Greece A three-year loan agreed by troika	€ 45 billion only the first year	2/3 from EU Bilateral loans from euro area Member States	1/3 from IMF	Hidden financial commitments were announced and the public debt increased	Fiscal and banking reform
2 May 2010	Greece	€ 110 billion for the other two years				
7 May 2010	**E**uropean **F**inancial **S**tability **F**acility (EFSF)	€ 750 billion for three years, 2010-2013	EU	1/3 from IMF	A temporary bailout mechanism	
22 November 2010	Ireland Requested access to the EFSF	€ 85 billion	2/3 from EU	1/3 from IMF	Banks over-leveraged over the real-estate boom in Ireland	A comprehensive examination of the banking system
23 March 2011	European Stability Mechanism (ESM)	€ 500 billion from 2013	€ 80 billion from paid-in capital of Eurozone members		Eurozone's permanent bailout vehicle	
24-25 March 2011	Euro Plus Pact				A stricter Stability and Growth Pact designed by Germany and France	
6 April 2011	Portugal requested access to the ESFS	€ 78 billion	2/3 from EU	1/3 from IMF	Omissions of public liabilities in the budget accounts	Portugal was asked to revise their public finances' figures and deal with the budget deficit and public debt

October 2011	Extension of the ESFS to:	a further € 440 billion				
26-27 Oct. 2011	Greece, A new aid package	€ 130 billion	ESFS		This measure aimed to calm the markets	
From Nov. 2011 to May 2012	Eurobonds Debate; Fiscal Compact;				As a permanent bailout mechanism	
9 June 2012	Spain requested access to ESM	€ 100 billion	EU A mix of bail-in (up to €45 billion) and bail-out	IMF	To support its banks	
2012	Italy, Only using the European Central Bank programmes					Italy was requested to do a fiscal reform by EU. IMF recommended a labour market reform; also pension reform.
16 March 2013	Cyprus	€ 10 billion	EU A mix of bail-in (up to €6.5 billion) and bail-out	IMF	To support the banks; The bail-in helped to protect the taxpayers as it affected the wealthiest, the most influential and the church	Cyprus was requested to do a banking reform; capital controls were fully lifted in 2015; in March 2016 Cyprus exited the adjustment programme
18 April 2013	Slovenia	$3.5 billion borrowed on international markets (5th May)			Managed to save its banks without a bailout from the ESM	

4.7 Conclusions

To sum up, the Federal Reserve and the ECB undertook differing paths of monetary easing in 2008, and the US growth and inflation appeared to respond more quickly to the measures, while the EZ area suffered a longer period of low growth – low inflation (see Table 4.4 below). Since the second half of 2016, the European economies have seen an upsurge in their activities and a slight increase in inflation, which is expected to continue through 2017, particularly the potential pressure on cost inflation as global production costs appear set to rise. This led to a similar debate in Europe about the path of asset holdings reduction that the ECB, and subsequently the ECB announced officially in October 2017 its plans to cut its monthly purchases from €60 billion to €30 billion from January 2018.

The conventional wisdom, for instance demonstrated in the BIS assessment of the impacts of the unconventional measures, suggests that the two central banks in the US and the EZ have been principally responsible for the economic recovery in both economic areas. As a major impact, particularly in the US (as also in the UK), has been the recovery of the stability and liquidity positions of the banks and other financial institutions, and, subsequently, a general increase in asset prices, particularly in the US then a degree of success has been achieved.

The factor that did make a substantial difference in the US was the existence of a Treasury and a federal fiscal budget. In the recession, automatic welfare stabilizers – social insurance benefits of various kinds – immediately kicked in. It is also the case that there was more fiscal freedom permitted constitutionally and in practice for the states of the USA than in the case of the EZ member states. This issue is also explored in Chapter 5 on regional imbalances. The

Obama administration wanted to extend fiscal intervention through government investment in infrastructure, but these measures were denied by Congress. Despite this, the overall economic welfare held up better in the US than the EU, which lacked a Treasury/Finance Ministry and a federal budget.

Our other finding is that both the US and Europe under-performed in countering the greatest financial crisis since 1929 because macroeconomic policy from 2008 became a combination of an expansionary monetary policy and restrictive fiscal policy (austerity) This determined the quite extraordinary 'unconventional' policies, which mitigated the crisis to an extent, but switched the whole economic structure in a new direction, one that favoured holders of financial, capital and property assets. This re-direction of economic policy is now held by many to have ushered in a new rentier age with a resultant loss of economic welfare and life chances for the many.

Monetary-only policies have also singularly incapable of addressing the regional dimension of continental economies, especially in the light of the distortions described in this chapter. Monetary policy – nowadays the province of the central bank (i.e. the Federal Reserve Board and the European Central Bank) – is *centralized*. Though there will be information provided via regional agents and perhaps discussion of the regional impacts of the central setting of the interest rate (Fed Funds Rate and ECB Repo Rate), the assessment of the need for rate changes, open market operations, credit easing (CE), and quantitative easing (QE) will be made in relation to the overall state of the economy, i.e. centrally. This raises the immediate question of a regional democratic deficit and the potential for socio-economic maldistribution across the economic area concerned. We return to this issue in the next chapter.

Federal Central Banks

Finally, the table below indicates, in summary form, the monetary and macro-economic impacts of the unconventional measures taken following the GFC.

Table 4.4: Impacts of the CE and QE Measures Taken

	FED QE programmes	ECB QE measures
QE large-scale asset purchases	$2.750 trillion	€2.086 trillion
Monthly purchases	$85 billion per month from Sept 2012 till Oct 2014	€80 billion per month from Sep 2016, reduced to €60 billion in April 2017
QE amounts	23% of US GDP	22% of EU GDP
FED Balance of sheet	$4.45 trillion (end-2016)	€3.66 trillion (end-2016)
Balance of sheet increased since 2008	**4 times and a half**	**2 times**
QE rounds impact on interest rate	2.5% point cut	1% point cut
QE rounds impact on unemployment	Reduced by more than 1% point	n.a
QE rounds impact on inflation	Increased by 0.5% point	n.a
Bond purchases 10% of GDP	Median reduction effect on the yield: 55 basis points	Median reduction effect on the yield: 45 basis points
Domestic impact response to 25- basis point reduction in 'shadow' rates[13]	US policy shock	ECB policy shock
Stronger depreciation pressure on the currency	– 0.01%	– 0.02%
Real GDP growth	0.04 % points	0.01% points
Equity price inflation	Nearly 0.5% points	– 0.05% points
CPI Inflation	0.07% points	0.01% points
Credit to private sector (loosening credit)	0.03% points	0.025% points
Impact on oil prices	0.5% points	0.0% points

Catching-up (Macroeconomic indicators)		
GDP, % change on a previous year	2015- 2.2% 2016 – 1.8% Expected 2017 – 0.7%	2015 – 2% 2016 – 1.9% Expected 2017 – 2%
Unemployment rate	4.5%	9.5%
Inflation	Personal Consumption Expenditure Price Index (PCEPI) – March 2017: 1.83%; Ten Year Average – 1.58% Core PCEPI (ex. Food and energy) – March 2017: 1.56%; Ten Year Average – 1.61% Median inflation rate across PCE categories – March 2017: 2.16%; Ten Year Average – 1.96%	Harmonised Index of Consumer Prices: Euro-area (19 countries) – March 2017: 0.8% 2016 – 0.2% European Union (28 countries) – March 2017: 0.6% 2016 – 0.3%
Interest rates	Federal Funds Target Rate – the range: [0.75%- 1.00%] of March 2017 [1.00% -1.25%] of June 2017 [1.25%-1.50%] of December 2017	Main Refinancing Operations, MRO – 0%; Deposit Facility Rate – (–0.4%)

Addendum

Table 4.5: Audited Annual Financial Statements of the Federal Reserve System (million $) as of 31 December 2016, 2015

Balance Sheet	2016	2015
Assets		
Gold certificates	$11,037	$11,037
Special drawing rights certificates	5,200	5,200
Coin	1,873	1,890
Loans	63	115

Federal Central Banks

System open market account:		
Treasury securities, net (of which $25,195 and $18,960 is lent as of Dec 31st 2016, and 2015 respectively	$2,567,422	$2,580,676
Government-sponsored enterprise debt securities, net (of which $44 and $146 is lent as of Dec. 31 2016 and 2015 respectively	16,648	33,748
Federal agency and government-sponsored enterprise mortgage-backed securities, net	$1,795,003	$1,800,449
Foreign currency denominated investments, net	19,442	19,567
Central bank liquidity swaps	5,563	997
Accrued interest receivable	25,598	25,418
Other assets	8	14
Investments held by consolidated variable interest entity (of which $1,742 and $1,778 is measured at fair value as of December 31, 2016 and 2015, respectively)	1,742	1,778
Bank premises and equipment, net	2,564	2,603
Items in process of collection	118	210
Other assets	1,056	1,063
Total assets	**$4,453,337**	**$4,484,765**
Liabilities and capital		
Federal Reserve Notes outstanding, net	$1,462,939	$1,379,551
System Open Market Account:		
Securities sold under agreements to repurchase	725,210	712,401
Other Liabilities	1,012	508
Liabilities of consolidated variable interest entity (of which $32 and $21 is measured at fair value as of December 31, 2016 and 2015, respectively)	33	57
Deposits:		
Depositary institutions	$1,759,676	$1,977,166
Treasury, general account	399,190	333,447
Other deposits	58,413	36,532
Interest payable to depository institutions and others	403	252

Accrued benefit costs	3,118	2,892
Deferred credit items	922	246
Accrued remittances to the Treasury	1,725	1,953
Other liabilities	255	252
Total liabilities	**$4,412,895**	**$4,445,257**
Capital paid-in	30,442	29,508
Surplus (including accumulated other comprehensive loss of $3,985 and $3,802 at December 31, 2016 and 2015, respectively)	10,000	10,000
Total capital	40,442	39,508
Total liabilities and capital	$4,453,337	$4,484,765

Table 4.6: Eurosystem Liquidity Situation (EUR billions), March 2017

	26th Oct – 24th Jan 2017	Increase/Decrease	27th July 2016 – 25th Oct 2016
Liabilities – liquidity needs			
Autonomous Liquidity factors	1,944.80	+28.1	1,916.70
Banknotes in circulation	1,110.50	+14.9	1,095.50
Government deposits	152.00	+0.1	151.90
Other autonomous factors	682.30	+13.0	669.30
Monetary Policy Instruments			
Current accounts	867.80	+105.80	762.00
Minimum reserve requirements	118.00	+0.8	117.20
Deposit facility	437.10	+67.20	369.90
Liquidity-absorbing fine-tuning operations	0.0	+0.0	0.0
Assets-Liquidity supply			

Federal Central Banks

Autonomous Liquidity factors	1,070.00	-56.2	1,126.20
Net foreign assets	681.50	-4.7	686.30
Net assets denominated in euro	388.40	-51.5	439.90
Monetary Policy Instruments			
Open market operations	2,179.90	+257.20	1,922.70
Tender operations	563.20	+29.70	533.50
MROs	34.3	-6.4	40.6
Three-month LTROs	13.30	-6.1	19.30
TLTRO-I	47.20	-13.10	60.30
TLTRO-II	468.50	+55.20	413.20
Outright portfolios	1,616.70	+227.40	1,389.20
First covered bond purchase programme	13.10	-2.80	15.90
Second covered bond purchase programme	7.0	-0.4	7.40
Third covered bond purchase programme	202.70	+11.20	191.60
Securities markets programme	102.20	-4.9	107.10
Asset-backed securities purchase programme	22.40	+1.90	20.50
Public sector purchase programme	1,221.20	+198.20	1,023.00
Corporate sector purchase programme	48.00	+24.20	23.90
Marginal lending facility	0.2	+0.1	0.1
Other liquidity-based information			
Aggregate liquidity needs	993.20	+85.20	908.00
Autonomous factors	875.20	+84.30	790.80
Excess liquidity	1,186.70	+172.00	1,014.70

Notes

1. The purchases were open-ended when announced. Then the Federal Reserve started to decrease the amount of asset purchases in January 2014, and eventually halted the purchases in October 2014.
2. Gavyn Davies, 'The end of global QE is fast approaching', FT (26 March 2017).
3. 'US Federal Reserve calls historic end to quantitative easing', FT (20 September 2017).
4. Baranova Y., Liu Z., Noss J., 'The role of collateral in supporting liquidity', Bank of England, Staff Working Paper No 609 (August 2016).
5. Infante, S., 'Money for Nothing: The Consequences of Repo Re-hypothecation', Federal Reserve Board, (September 2014).
6. The purchases were supposed open-ended and unlimited in size when they were announced, but the facility has never been activated.
7. ECB, Economic Bulletin, Issue 1 and 2, (2017).
8. Fratzscher, M., M Lo Duca and R. Straub, 'On the international spillovers of US quantitative easing', DIW Discussion Papers, no 1304, (2013).
9. Fratzscher, M., M Lo Duca and R. Straub, 'ECB Unconventional Monetary Policy Actions: Market Impact, international Spillovers and Transmission Channels', Paper presented at the 15th Jacques Polak Annual Research Conference of the International Monetary Fund, (2013).
10. Chen Q., Marco Lombardi, A. Ross and Feng Zhu 'Global impact of US and euro area unconventional monetary policies: a comparison', BIS Working Papers, No 610 (2017).
11. Gagnon J., 'Quantitative Easing: An underappreciated success', PB16-4, Peterson Institute of International Economics (2016).
12. Mario Draghi, 'Monetary Policy: Past, Present and Future', speech at the Frankfurt European Banking Congress, 20 Nov. 2015.
13. Shadow interest rates are constructed by estimation of a dynamic factor model on a large set of variables

Chapter 5

Regional Inequalities, Federalism, and the Dynamics of Property Markets. US and EU Compared

5.1 Federalism, Central Banking, and Regional Economic Disparities

At first sight it might be assumed that federalism in its political and central banking form would mitigate regional disparities. This was an issue that animated the authors of this report, especially since the question did not appear to have received much research.[1] The issue was also provoked by the responses to the GFC. Had credit easing and quantitative easing benefitted some geographical areas more than others? In Europe the answer was only too painfully obvious. Responses to the global financial crisis had led to devastation and prolonged periods of austerity. All the major

European banks were in crisis and 2009 was a brutal time for all the major economies. Thereafter the northern economies recovered far more rapidly than the southern European economies. We think that a federal political system should seek to mitigate as much as possible such divergence. Of course the European Union is a confederation whereas the United States is a federal state. At the level of economic policy this difference matters, and we pursue this in chapters 6 and 7.

The idea that moves to federation would lead to the reduction of regional disparities is very much a European idea and part of the European project. Not only would the EEC bind the large industrial nations of northern Europe inseparably together but it would bring growth and prosperity to the impoverished periphery: southern Italy, Greece, Spain, Portugal and Ireland. The European Union has always had a strong regional policy, involving large transfers of development and infrastructure funds to the less developed regions. This policy reached its highpoint under Jacques Delors, when it was an explicit policy that the move to a Single Market would be balanced by a strong regional policy (Cohesion Fund).[2] Against that, however, is the new dynamic set up by a common currency zone and the ECB regime. A low single interest rates across the European economic area led to an investment boom – dangerously speculative – in the peripheral regions. In GDP terms this indicated a narrowing of disparities, but these gains were sharply reversed by the austerity policies enforced following the GFC. This chapter examines – aside from explicit regional policies – the positive and negative impacts of capital flows and the recycling of savings surpluses made feasible by the single market and the common currency.

From the North American perspective, there is no necessary assumption that federalism must lead to the equalization of the economic fortunes of regions and particular states. The Canadian federal system builds in particularism and divergence to an extent, as a feature of the autonomy of provinces. The varying economic geography of Canada throws together regions rich in resources, regions with low populations and few resources as well as four or five very large prosperous cities. Canada has an effective country-wide welfare state in place and this automatically provides transfers from those of high income to those at points of low income, and to the extent income inequalities sometimes align with differences between federal states, then transfer payments to poorer regions takes place automatically; this, ignoring the specific transfer of regional funds for development.

The same argument applies to the United States. The state of Alabama is proud of its difference to the north, and it is not overly envious of the richer states in the Union. That said, two-thirds of U.S. revenue is collected at federal level, and a large proportion of individual state's budget derives from federal expenditure and transfers. In contrast, EU states received only a half to three and half percent (of their GDP) from EU funds.

The European idea of federation as part of process of regional aid and equalization of life chances is based on the normative value of solidarity, again so much stressed by Jacques Delors. We don't have to return to de Tocqueville to realize that the value system of the USA is based on individualism bordering on atomism, not solidarity. So, the expectations with regard to regional disparities are higher in Europe than in North America, but federal redistribution is far greater in the US. (The entry of previously eastern bloc states in the EU has altered the normative consensus on solidarity and welfare; for eastern EU members maintenance of newly acquired nation-state sovereignty is more important.)

Having noted the different normative expectations, academic research reveals some common underlying mechanisms. Once a common currency area is created, a number of dynamics are made possible. In a political federation population flows, mainly migration from poor to richer regions, occurs. Also, investment flows and movement of capital to regions previously unconsidered occur when single market conditions are put in place.

We present some of the results of our initial research that explain the processes of both convergence and divergence.

In a seminal paper in 1992, Barro & Xavier[3] established that in the period 1880 to 1980 there had been an overall convergence between rich and poor areas in the USA. Incomes between rich and poor states converged at around 1.8% a year. In the longer term this adds up to a considerable narrowing of differentials, and represents a significant catch up by the poorer states with their richer rivals.

Data on income differentials qualify this conclusion. If we make the assumption that lower income populations are clustered in certain states, for example some southern states of the US, then increasing income differentials indicate an increase in regional disparity. This assumption is countered by examples such as Washington DC, where despite high income inequality Washington comes out in the data as a rich state. Hence income differential data is standing in (for want of better research) for differences in income level of states.

**Chart 5.1: USA Maximum & Minimum Per
Capita Disposable Income 2009 US$**

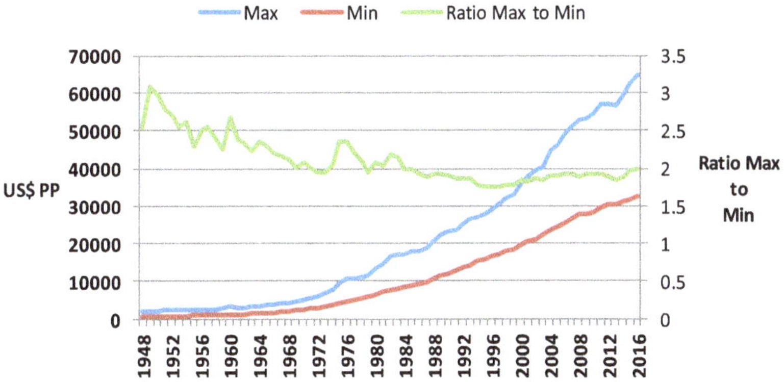

Source: BEA & Author's Calculations. The Green line shows the ratio
between highest and lowest per capita income dropped from around
3 in the 1940's to around 2 in 216. Since the early 1980s the ratio has
hovered around 2. It appears to be on a slightly upward trend again.

These trends are shown in chart 5.1 for the period 1948 to
2016. Both the maximum and minimum disposable incomes
rose over the period 1948 to 2016. Minimum incomes increased
more rapidly up to the 1980s, after which maximum incomes
began to rise more rapidly. Thus, indicating that the catch-up
effect by the poorer regions has effectively ceased (see Ganong
& Shoag, 2015).[4] The ratio between maximum and minimum
income levels (green line) fell until the 1980s, and levelled off
and increasing slightly, particularly in the post GFC period.

Chart 5.2 tells a similar story over a longer period of
time. The share of the top 1% income earners in total income
reached a peak in 1929, and then fell into a long secular
decline until the 1980s. Reaganomics and further economic
de-regulation reversed this trend. As the chart shows, the
share of income of the top 1% is now back to where it was at
the beginning of the twentieth century.

Chart 5.2: USA: Share of top 1% in income (exc capital gains).

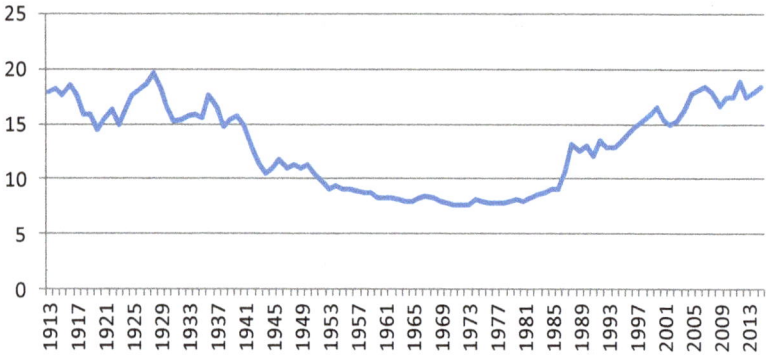

Source: www.chartbookofeconomicinequality.com by Anthony B.
Atkinson, Joe Hasell, Salvatore Morelli, and Max Roser, 2017.

This has social, economic and political implications. It suggests that after taking other factors into account, income differentials between regions within the USA have started to diverge, meaning that the rich areas get richer, and the poor get poorer relative to a national average. At this point another important trend comes into play. With an absence or strong reduction in internal migration, and in particular from poor to richer areas, earlier safety 'valves' allowing citizens to take advantage of the American dream may also have largely ceased.

The next question is to try and establish why this might have happened? And of relevance for this study, has the Federal Reserve in any way contributed to this outcome? Our provisional answer to this is that there have been developments in the property market that have hindered internal migration. And that this has been strongly influenced by the actions of the Federal Reserve.

5.2 Internal Migration in the USA and Property Prices

Ganong and Shoag (2017) suggested a mechanism that contributed to the throttling back of internal migration within the USA. And it comes through the combination of interest rate policies, and steps to lower lender risk in the US property market.

In the convergence period (1880 to 1980), higher productivity and wages attracted migrants from lower income states to higher income areas. Traditionally this was seen in terms of an emigration out of the South and towards northern industrial cities. More recently flows out of the centre of the country towards the coastal regions have also happened. And even more recently there are flows towards areas such as to the South (a reversal of the earlier pattern), the South West and towards the Rockies (Colorado and the Dakotas).[5]

The supply of property and residential housing was reasonably responsive to inflows of labour before the 1980s. And increased competition for jobs may have helped to lower the rates of wage increases in higher income areas, while through reduced competition for jobs in the poorer states may have helped raise wages for those who stayed behind.

Moreover, the demand for housing in high income areas up to the 1980s was encouraged by lower interest rates on residential mortgages, and by other risk reducing measures (including federal subsidies) to effectively lower the cost of housing for immigrants.

Various parts of the US have zoning laws restricting new housing development, sometimes quite severely. Ganong and Shoag claim that the net effect of zoning laws and tougher building regulations has been to reduce the supply of new housing in higher income areas.[6] And this in turn has meant that while skilled labour can still afford to move into higher income areas, unskilled labour faces greater obstacles. Whereas housing costs for a skilled lawyer in NY form around 21% of a lawyer's disposable income, they form around 52% of an unskilled janitor.

On top of this, interest rates that are effectively set too low to manage supply and demand in the housing market, plus building and zoning restrictions have led to an upward spiral in house prices in high income areas, thus 'capitalizing' the gain in housing assets for incumbents. This in turn has contributed to a worsening of income and wealth equality within the Union. (See also chart 5.4 below).

Chart 5.3: Internal labour migration affected by housing costs and prices in the US

Household Level: Housing Share of Income
MSA Fixed Effects

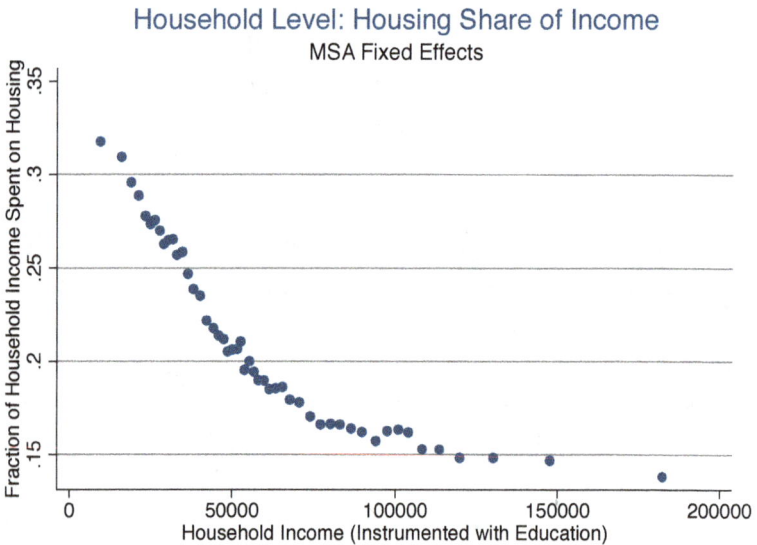

Household Income (Instrumented with Education)

Chart 5.3 shows how the share of housing costs in household income rises as incomes fall. For the very poorest households, housing costs form over 30% of household income, compared with around 5% for the very richest.

The traditional approach towards interest rates in economics has concentrated attention on investment as a means of expanding capacity in the economy. There is considerable empirical research suggesting that these linkages are of minor importance. Corporate investment decisions are only marginally affected by policy led short run interest rates.[7]

The substantially more important financial flows in the economy are loans to the household sector for consumption purposes made by the banking sector. And the main use of such loans is to buy property. Property purchase decisions are influenced by interest rate decisions as has been shown by Himmelberg (2005) and Sutton and Agnes Subelyte (2017).[8] Himmelberg's evidence suggested that a 1% decline in short term (i.e. policy led) interest rates could raise house prices by between 19 and 33% over a 3-year period. Sutton and Agnes Subelyte's evidence points to a more modest 5% rise in house prices following a 1% fall in short term interest rates.

The argument outlined above illustrates how falling interest rates, caused substantially by GFC related dislocations following the sub-prime crisis of 2007/8, have ultimately led to higher property prices. This reduced the rate of immigration into the richer areas, and rewarded incumbent property owners with windfall gains, adding to their wealth. This in turn led to a widening of income and wealth differentials within the USA, and could be said to have thereby weakened the state of the Union.

There is further evidence of growing income differentials emerging in the 1980s and continuing to the present. Chart 5.4 below shows how the situation had developed by 2016.

Chart 5.4: US States Disposable Personal Income US$ per person pa. 2016

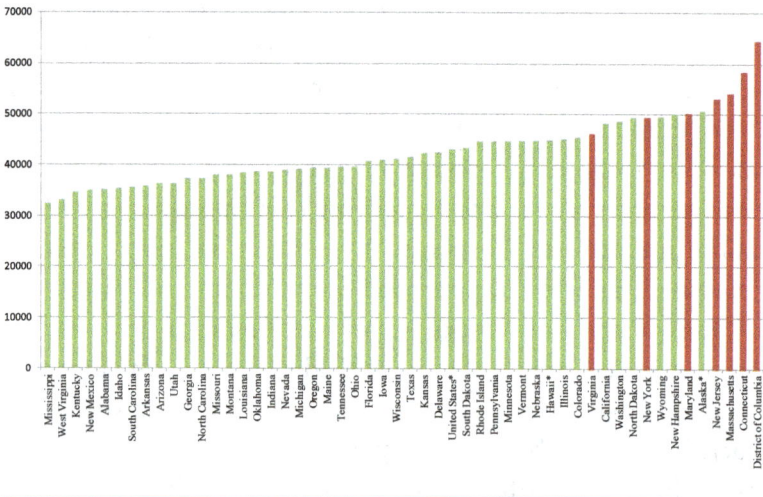

Source: BEA. States marked in red are in the North East

As can be seen the states in the North and North East of the country are now the richest in the country. There is evidence that this occurred concurrently with the large expansion of the financial sector, despite the GFC in 2007/8. It is possible that the negative impact of the GFC on the rest of the country was more severe than on the financial sector itself, although further work is needed to provide evidence for this.

While certainly not exhaustive, the charts suggest that income differentials have widened since 1980. The rates of migration from poorer to richer areas have fallen. States located close to the federal government appear to have performed better, and incomes are higher than in the rest of the country. And these trends have hardened. Whereas in 1948 the high-income states were distributed across all main regions, by 2016, high incomes are increasingly associated

with the North/North East. As those states prospered, the
states in the Mid West – e.g. Ohio, Pennsylvania and associated with heavy engineering – have performed worse.

The exact role played by the central bank in this development is far from clear. Our hypothesis is that financial
de-regulation may have led to a greater concentration of
income in the North and North East, in other words in those
places where the power of finance was always strong. They
appear to have benefited from central bank policies more
than other parts of the country. The more surprising element
to this is that despite the GFC, those areas close to Washington DC and New York appear to have performed better.

Given the results of the last Presidential election, and
the earlier rise in the politically and economically conserv-
ative Tea Party, the regional trends shown above are creating
political waves, and undermining confidence in the ability of
the Union to deliver growth and prosperity that is evenly and
fairly distributed across the USA. And this in turn creates a
challenge to the Federal Reserve, that may well have to pay
closer attention to the distributional consequences of its
economic policies than was previously the case.

5.3 Regional Inequalities and Eurozone Membership

The European context is still in flux and lacks the *institutional*
stability long since achieved by the United States. While
the US is currently experiencing a reduction in internal
migration and labour mobility, historically the levels have
always been higher than in the EU. To cite the Bulgarian
economist and ex-Finance Minister, Simeon Djankov,
'Unlike in Europe, there is capital and labour mobility in the
United States as well significant federal transfers. Twenty-

nine percent of Americans live and work outside the state in which they were born. Only 3 percent of Europeans live in another EU country.'[9]

Turning now to inequalities, both the EU and the Eurozone have wider income differentials than the USA. The differences between the richer states and the poorer states is greater in the EU/EZ. It is therefore more important for the Eurozone to show that being a member of the zone will be associated with converging incomes per capita, so that the poorer countries effectively catch up with the richer ones.

In the USA this process, which as we have seen has largely come to a halt, was encouraged by the use of Federal level fiscal transfer payments. There is a federal pension (retirement) system that provides some protection to the elderly across the entire country. There is also Federal social insurance and unemployment insurance as well as Medicaid, which act as transfer payments from the rich to the poor.

The EU/EZ does not currently have any EU/EZ wide fiscal transfer programmes, other than regional assistance 'cohesion' funds and subsidy payments to farmers across the Union as part of the Common Agricultural Policy. This differs from the situation *within* EU member states, most of whom have well developed fiscal transfer systems. The difficulty here being that this does not help to eliminate the difference in average national incomes *between* member states.

**Chart 5.5: For EU, long "tail" of low income countries: Average value
100. EU GDP Income per cap @ PPP rates 2016 % EU average**

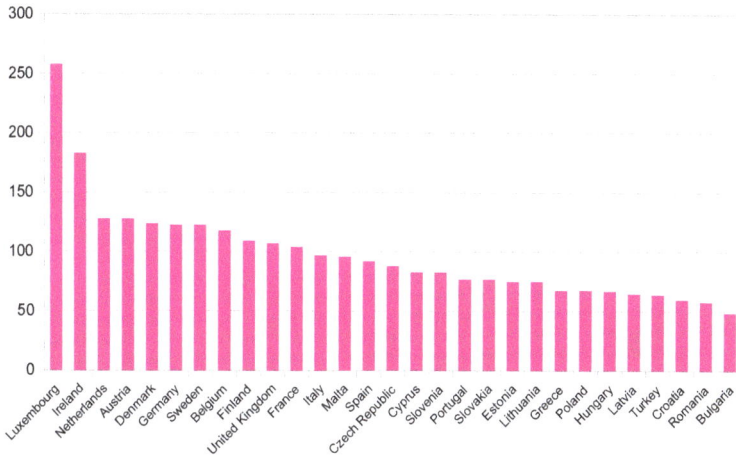

Chart 5.5 compares member state per capita average income expressed as a proportion of the EU average. If the simple EU average is 100, then the member states' income ranges from 258 to just less than 50 (which is half the EU average). There is a long tail of lower income member states.

The poorer parts of the EU are located in the East and in the South. The wealthier areas are in the North and West. Italy and Spain are the two largest Mediterranean countries with below average per capita incomes. And this rather highlights the point that with the exception of Ireland, all the other EU member states encountering serious financial difficulties post GFC are located in the poorer South. Of the original 'western' members of the Eurozone, Greece now has the lowest per capita incomes, 25% below the EU average.

Chart 5.6: Eurozone Countries marginally wealthier. Average value: 105 Eurozone GDP Income per cap @ PPP rates 2016 % EU average

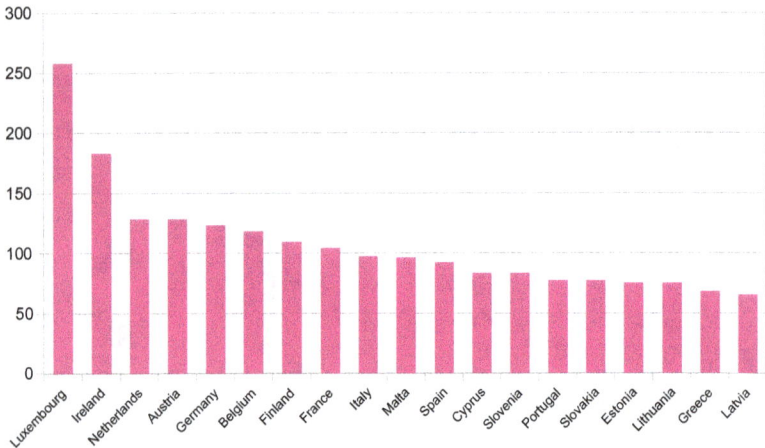

How does the Eurozone compare with the EU? Chart 5.6 shows that the Eurozone average is estimated at 105 of the EU level – The EZ is therefore richer than the EU as a whole. The richest EZ members on a per capita basis are Luxembourg – owing to a very favourable tax regime, Ireland – also benefiting from lower taxes, the Netherlands, Austria and then Germany. The less well-off EZ member states are in the East, with Latvia currently having the lowest per capita income. The range of per capita income is slightly less in the EZ than for the EU as a whole. The differences between rich and poor in both the EU and the EZ are more pronounced than they are in the US – even though on other individual measures of household income, the US is a more unequal society than the EU.

The current structure of the ECB is built up on the basis of national CBs. These 'meso' level organizations will need to think carefully about the current income differentials between member states. Over time it is reasonable to expect that these differences will narrow. This process might well be accelerated were the ECB to incorporate more specific regional financial and economic targets in its charter. This is one of our recommendations (see Conclusion).

5.4 CB Policy & Regional Impacts in the EU/Eurozone

The Federal Reserve operates in a financial system and structure that has been in place for some time. The position of the ECB in the Eurozone is very different. It is explicitly part of a project to bring about 'ever closer union' within the EU, not just the Eurozone. While this is frequently over-looked in the UK, it is worth recalling that with the exception of the UK (soon to leave the EU), and Denmark, all other member states are committed to join the Euro at some point in the future. In joining the Euro, all member states are committing themselves to the criteria of the Maastricht Treaty – that member states should not have public sector deficits greater than 3% of GDP, and public sector debt no more than 60% of GDP. These are goals recently signed up to by Poland, even though Poland is not part of the Eurozone.[10] Thus the regions are being sucked into a form of monetary and fiscal centralization.

This 'functionalist' approach to integration has, however, been disrupted by political and financial crises. As the ECB was taking shape, simultaneously a number of East European countries completing their transition from being satellites of the former Soviet Union were now joining the EU. In some cases, these countries such as the Baltic states, Slovakia and Slovenia, were also joining the Eurozone. As documented in Chapter 4, the ECB was flat-footed in its response to the GFC and it was particularly uncaring about the economic health of eastern countries neighbouring the EZ. Simeon Djankov attributes this failure to Jean-Claude Trichet in particular, as the then Chair of the ECB.[11] The negative experience has not been forgotten by Hungary's Viktor Orbán.

Another point, not fully appreciated, is that the rapid series of events and accession of states did not eventuate in a uniform currency zone. The Eurozone is still work in progress, as can be seen by the patchwork quilt of membership across the European continent. The majority of member states are in Western Europe, representing the fact that monetary union came after years of patient negotiation and considerations – accelerated as a result of the post 1989 deals struck, notably between France and the re-united Germany. Monetary union and the surrender of the Deutschemark were the two concessions needed to gain the acquiescence to German reunification. They also reflect longer term concerns by the French government, not always shared by the French electorate, about building more robust, multilateral institutions within the EU as a way of limiting the hegemony of any one single member state. (See above Chapter 2.)

**Chart 5.7: Eurozone Members (Blue) 2017:
Something of a patchwork quilt**

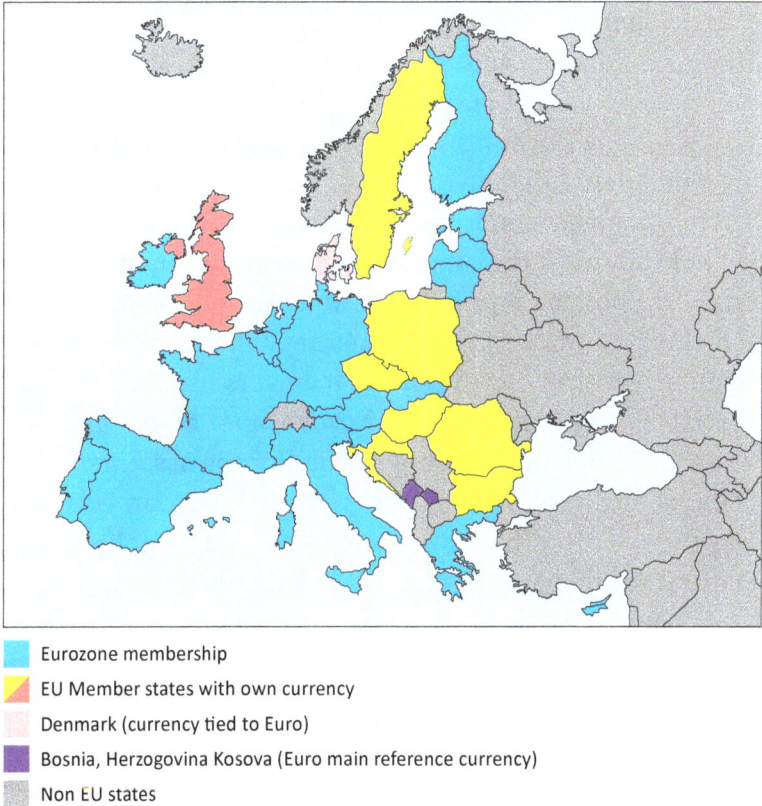

- Eurozone membership
- EU Member states with own currency
- Denmark (currency tied to Euro)
- Bosnia, Herzogovina Kosova (Euro main reference currency)
- Non EU states

For all that though there are several economically important countries that have either opted out, or have delayed their joining the Eurozone. The main one of these is the UK, whose significance in global financial markets is greater than its economic strength would suggest. Denmark, the other country opting out of the Euro, maintains a very close parity between the Danish Kroner and the Euro, well within the limits agreed as part of the earlier exchange rate mechanism. And Denmark has shown no great proclivities to resort to exchange rate changes to restore competitiveness in the same way that Britain has.

The other 'absent' countries include Sweden, Poland, the Czech Republic (but not its former other half, Slovakia), Hungary, Romania and Bulgaria. As discussed above, Poland now has a balanced budget policy, so would be able to join the Euro. The positions of Hungary, Romania and Bulgaria are somewhat different.

Hungary's economic performance, while improving, may yet not fully meet the conditions for membership. This is also true for Romania and Bulgaria. It is also the case that the remaining countries in the former republic of Yugoslavia are also not yet ready for Eurozone membership. These include Serbia, Bosnia-Herzegovina, Kosovo and Macedonia. For some countries membership of the Euro is associated with being at the 'top table' in terms of the European economic league table. It is broadly regarded as being a political and cultural advantage to be part of the Eurozone.

A relevant factor for smaller countries, notably the Baltic states, is that being a member of the Eurozone – and thus surrendering control over currency decisions – is a blessing rather than a curse. Small countries cannot, by themselves, exercise much influence over what their more powerful neighbours do. As the Deutschemark currency zone emerged during the 1970s to 1990s, so it became apparent that other member countries could not influence German policy to any tangible degree, and simply had to go along with it. Being a member of the Eurozone does at least mean the smaller member states are consulted about, and have a small degree of influence over policy changes. They are not being dictated to as under earlier arrangements. And for many smaller countries, this is just fine.

So while not all EU member states are part of the Euro, it is true to say that they are all affected by it, and will orientate their economic affairs to take account of this. And whatever other disadvantages the Euro might be seen to have, its very existence removes one of the risks to the governments of smaller states that they will effectively be forced into accepting economic arrangements decided upon by their larger neighbours, with possibly significant negative effects on their own economies. Some would view this as a gain, rather than a loss of sovereignty. (We omit discussion of the UK's tortured stance on this issue.)

5.5 ECB Policy and Property Prices

The crucial role of interest rates and the property sector has already been discussed in the context of the Fed and the US economy. And it has been established that the impact of falling interest rates was to accelerate the recovery in property prices post GFC in many, but not all parts of the country, and this has curtailed the movement of labour from poorer to richer areas.

How have interest rate changes affected property prices in the EU? The situation varies across the member states, and this partly reflects the different ways in which property purchases are funded. It is also a function of the different proportions of public sector housing on offer – often with controlled rents – and that of the private sector. Within the private sector there are differences between outright property ownership, and renting, with various forms of consumer protection. Thus care is needed in interpreting the statistics.

The second point to bear in mind is given the close relationship between central banks, commercial banks and the ECB, this represents an area where the ECB cannot afford to fail. Its primary objective, not to forget, is to maintain price stability, and this also has to include price stability in the property market, particularly since this is so strongly affected by changes in interest rates. Hence, the performance of property markets within the Eurozone (EZ) is an important test case for the ability of the ECB to carry out its role in maintaining the stability of the financial system.

For all the ECB's other successes in maintaining liquidity and in essentially eliminating retail price inflation as a policy issue, its record with respect to property prices is highly questionable.

The following rather sweeping generalization captures the essence of the situation. Richer northern countries with growing populations of pensioners as well as colder climates, led a demand for holidays and retirement homes in warmer sunnier climes. This was also a convenient way for banks in the Northern countries to lend on the surpluses they were earning.

In the 'noughties', German and French banks lent on to their partner banks in countries like Italy, Spain and Greece, who in turn lent funds to households to buy properties. In the immediate aftermath of the establishment of the Euro and the ECB there was a period of interest rate convergence. This meant that in many smaller countries now part of the EZ, interest rates, and particularly longer-term interest rates, fell rapidly, converging on those of the 'anchor' nation, Germany.[12] With the benefit of hindsight it looks increasingly clear that this, in addition to other factors, helped to spark off a significant property boom in a number of EZ countries. The most affected were Ireland, Greece, and Spain. This is shown in Chart 5.8 below.

**Chart 5.8: Property Prices PIIGS in S.Europe.
Annual % change net of CPI change**

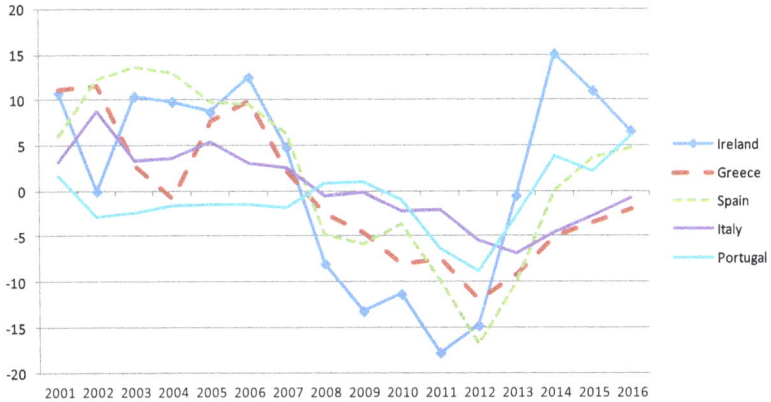

Even within this group of EZ member states there were
some striking differences. Property prices in Portugal and
Italy were less volatile than in the other countries, although
in both there was a general tendency for prices to fall from
2008 to 2014. So, in contrast to the USA, falling interest
rates did not uniformly lead to higher property prices across
the EZ.

Chart 5.9: Price Changes in Property Annual Rate of change relative to Consumer Price changes EU & Eurozone (EZ)

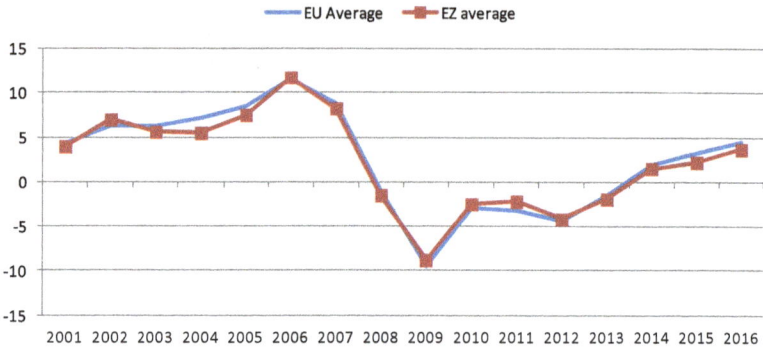

Taking a step back, it can be seen in Chart 5.9 what the simple average price changes for the EU and EZ in property prices have been in the period leading up the GFC EU property prices were increasing by around 5% a year, somewhat greater than the rate of increase in the EZ. During and after the GFC prices declined quite steeply in both the EU/EZ (-10%). There then followed 4 years of further price declines, before a slow recovery can be seen from 2014 onwards. Property price increases in the EU are rising faster than in the EZ. This may be largely due to the 'catch up' effects on property prices in Eastern Europe, as well as robust price increases in the UK. Chart 5.11 does not suggest that the EZ enjoyed better price discipline in residential property than the EU as a whole.

There were old fashioned property boom in Spain, Portugal and Italy that pushed up property prices beyond the affordability of local residents, both in terms of purchase, as well as for renting purposes. It was all rather reminiscent of earlier excesses in the USA. Back in the

1920s property companies speculated on building on Florida swamps; in the 'noughties' the same thing was happening across Eire.

As the GFC unfolded, so the same problems arose in the EU as in the US. House purchasers were lulled into a false sense of security as interest rates progressively fell. When, in the light of the sovereign debt crisis, and the breakdown in inter member-state lending occurred, as well as consequent rising unemployment, purchasers could no longer service their loans. Those desperate enough to sell may have liquidated their assets at a fraction of their peak values. On other occasions, the banks foreclosed on the loans, adding yet more property to their assets, while having to write off the value of the loans.

Negative equity and debt foreclosures led to a collapse in property prices in some, but not all, EZ/EU countries. At the same time, as part of broader changes introduced to deal with various debt crises, governments, in a move to increase their tax revenues focused their attention on property owners, who were now vulnerable to depredations of the tax man, as they found the costs of property ownership started to spiral upwards – triggering off more defaults.

How is this reflected in the level of property prices as measured by a property price index? This provides a barometer of how far the value of property assets has risen or fallen, and therefore provides an indication of the extent of negative equity amongst households.

Chart 5.10 shows what happened to Portugal, Ireland, Italy, Greece and Spain, all countries that (with the exception of Italy) required various forms of bail out, either through the auspices of the ECB, EU and the IMF[13].

Chart 5.10: Property Price Index (net CPI) 2015=100. PIIGS S.Europe

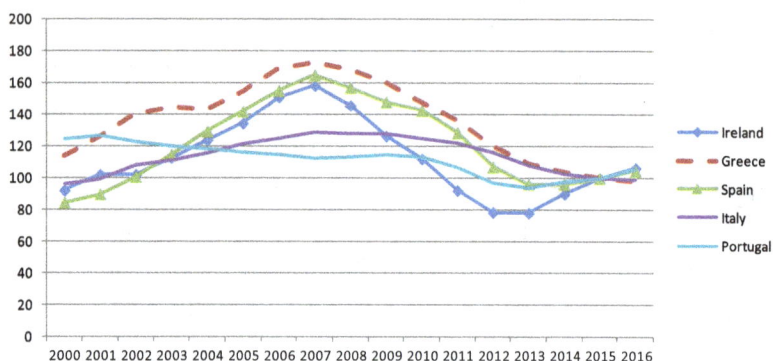

Property prices rose steeply in all countries, except Portugal in the run up to the GFC. The most rapid increases occurring in Ireland and Greece. This was then followed by a long period of falling property prices, from 2007 to 2014, before a minor recovery set in. To put this in perspective, it means that there was no appreciable gains in property value for anyone who bought and held property since the beginning of the century. Anyone who purchased property from 2003/4 onwards is sitting on capital losses of anything between 20 and 40%. in many southern European countries. These ongoing negative equity situations make it difficult/impossible for most property owners to move. And even though interest rates have been low (assuming the owner had a variable rate mortgage), other difficulties, such as rising unemployment, has led to loan defaults, and the acquisition of property assets by banks who foreclosed on the loans, which are probably earning the banks a negative return at the moment.

It also has to be considered that in the property market, the then general easing of capital restrictions, and local de-regulation among financial companies and banks, very probably added to the volatility in the property market.

While this may not be seen as the primary policy goal of the ECB, it is difficult to deny the charge that the ECB and the national CBs were negligent in monitoring and attempting to control the emerging asset price bubble in property. And this price bubble was a direct effect of widespread falls in interest rates as a result of the formation of the Euro, which led to what can be euphemistically be called a 'mispricing of risk'.

Chart 5.11 summarizes this situation. It compares the level of the property price index in the broader EU and the EZ. There has been substantially more volatility in property prices within the Eurozone than in the broader EU. And this was particularly true for the period 2000 to 2012. Property prices increased and then fell with much greater volatility than in the EU as a whole.

Chart 5.11: EU & EZ Property Price Index. 2015=100. Net of CPI

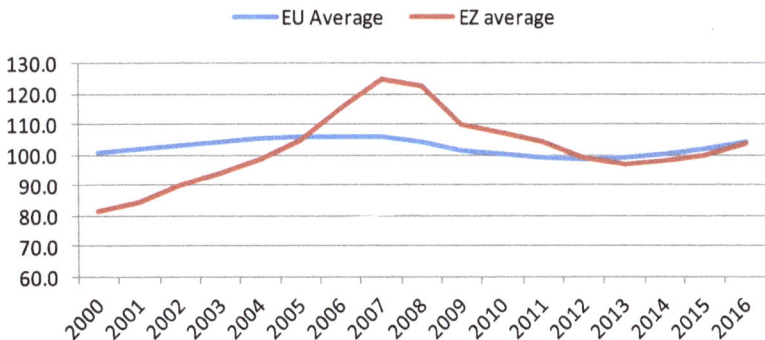

The post GFC recovery has been muted in both the EZ and the EU, although from a macro stability point of view, the bankers might argue that calmness has now returned to property – even if it is reminiscent of the calmness of the cemetery.

At the beginning of this chapter the point was made that the Eurozone (as indeed the EU) are works in progress. They have been subject to enormous institutional changes since the beginning of the century. And it may be that this is one of the defences most applicable to the ECB, which struggled with many of its policy hands tied behind its back, to maintain a semblance of order in the markets for financial assets, including property.

However, it is also true that, as in the US, the impact of QE is likely to result in increasing asset prices including property. There is already some evidence, as shown in charts 5.10 and 5.11, with the exception of Greece that a slow recovery of property prices has been occurring over the past 18 months. This will of course benefit those who have property and will disadvantage those who do not.

It may also be a testimony to the unfinished agenda facing the ECB and the EU. It will surely be desirable to avoid such wrenching changes in property prices in the future. As the example of the Fed shows, there is only so much the CBs can do in larger federal areas, although this appears to be true for national CBs too – *vide* the Bank of Japan in the 1980-90s and the Bank of England to this current day.

Notes

1. This oversight has been noted by the economic geographer Geoff Mann. See his 'Hobbes' Redoubt? Toward a geography of monetary policy', *Progress in Human Geography* 34(5), (2010), pp. 601-625.
2. David Marsh argues that the measures of the Cohesion Fund 'fell a long way short of the thoroughgoing fiscal redistribution for weaker regions of individual countries that is normally available within industrialised countries' national budgets' (*The Euro*, p. 148).

3. Barro, Robert J. and Xavier, Sala-i-Martin, 'Convergence', *Journal of Political Economy* 100 (2), 1992, pp. 223-251.

4. Peter Ganong and Daniel Shoag 'Why Has Regional Income Convergence in the U.S. Declined?' *Journal of Urban Economics* [Internet] 102 (2017), pp. 76-90.

5. Ganong & Shoah (2017), p. 29.

6. Ganong & Shoah (2017), p. 31, figure 1.

7. Ganong and Shoag (2017), pp. 76-90.

8. Charles Himmelberg, Christopher Mayer and Todd Sinai, 'Assessing High House Prices: Bubbles, Fundamentals, and Misperceptions', https://www.aeaweb. org/articles?id=10.1257/089533005775196769; Sinai, Todd and Nicholas Souleles, 'Owner Occupied Housing as a Hedge Against Rent Risk,' *Quarterly Journal of Economics* (May 2005).

9. Simeon Djankov, *Inside the Euro Crisis. An Eyewitness Account*, Peterson Institute for International Economics (2014), p. 13.

10. This is included in one of the protocols dealing with the ECB and 'excessive debt' attached to the Treaty of Lisbon.

11. Djankov, *Inside the Euro Crisis*, pp. 66-67.

12. German interest rates are the lowest in the Eurozone system.

13. It is notable though that all the countries, with the exception of Greece, struggled to free themselves from the indignities heaped on them by various 'troikas' of bankers demanding (and mostly getting) radical reforms and the imposition of austerity on the indebted countries. Ireland, Spain, and Portugal all sought to free themselves from the 'yoke' of the troika as soon as was practical. It would be hard to imagine an American state seeking to free itself from the clutches of the Fed in a similar situation.

Chapter 6
Federal Responses to the Global Financial Crisis

The Euro is generally referred to as a common currency, but should it not be thought of as a federal currency? It is not a national currency, for it abolished currency borders within the EZ. Its design, if not its planning, was aimed at achieving integration at the federal level. Its supporters were reasonably clear that after its introduction, at some point, the accompanying federal institutions – a federal exchequer and a federal state – would be created, if not voluntarily then out of necessity. The necessity lies is the fact that all fiat currencies have to be owned by a state which is responsible for it; common usage is not its defining feature.

To an extent it was logical that the designers of the ECB created an institution that was less than a fully-fledged federal central bank, because Europe's political and legal system remained confederal. The ECB was supra-national but not federal, though it was in charge of a currency that had all the attributes of federal money. Giscard d'Estaing, past French finance minister and past French President, recognized the issue well enough, and it was his hand that drafted a European federal constitution in 2003-4. The Convention for the Future of Europe sought to create the attributes of a federal state: a full-time President, and foreign minister, an army and police force. The Convention met with widespread lack of enthusiasm by national electorates and rejection in a referendum by the otherwise pro-European Denmark.

As already recounted here, and elsewhere, the ECB's primary function was oriented to keeping price inflation within a target range. If one goes back to the preparations made by Otto Pöhl at the Bundesbank and Commissioner Delors, there was unanimity that the ECB was going to be an engine of enforcement: tight money, fiscal discipline, low retail price inflation and international market competitiveness.[1] However the war against inflation was already being won *before* this mighty engine had been fired up: energy was cheaper, commodities from Asian markets and new WTO members *all helped to lower global* inflation.

For the Bundesbank inflation was, to recall, always a monetary problem. The resulting ECB was, in the new context of the late 1990s, a deflation machine in its monetary policies. *But* the ECB was no longer solely in control of money and credit creation. Neither was the ECB in control, in a regulatory sense, of European banks and international banks based in Europe. There was no money border between the EZ and London, Hong Kong, Tokyo and New York. There was no European bank insurance scheme, just as the ECB itself had no emergency plans as a lender of last resort. These features were outside and excluded from its charter.

So, when we turn to the build-up of leveraged debt in the 2000s and the reaction of the ECB to the GFC in 2007, we see an abandonment – or rather a working around – many of its rules. And European national economic and financial ministries scrambled to rush through joint 'solutions' and in doing so they created ad hoc institutions that departed from the legal framework of confederation. As predicted by Delors, Kohl et al, something would have to emerge to handle what turned out to be a combined banking, financial and sovereign-nation crisis. Emergency funds and ancillary committees were transformed into a quasi-Treasury and executive federal bodies.

Chapter 4 (Central Banks Responses to the GFC) demon-strates not the similarity but an equivalence of the measures taken in the US and in the EZ. The United States was more effective in its reactions to the GFC because it had federal institutions in place. Europe was forced, up to a point, into federal solutions but was handicapped by its need to improvise its institutional delivery.

The speed and decisiveness of *federal* monetary *author-ities* is critical in a banking crisis. The US Treasury in full crisis mode recapitalised the banking system by $431 billion within weeks of the meltdown. Banks and insurance companies were taken into government administration, others were merged, shareholders given haircuts. The short-term money markets, dominated by a hugely expanded money mutual funds, had to be instantly rescued through the use of short term bills. Bad financial assets were purchased by the Federal Reserve, underwritten by Treasury, so much so that the Fed's balance sheet tripled in size. The target federal find rate was dropped to zero, followed by quantitative easing (as described in Chapter 4).[2] The politics of this was highly contentious, but Treasury acted legally and an angry Congress acceded – eventually – to the measures. Federal executive and federal democracy worked together, even if not harmoniously.

The ECB acted with alacrity cutting its interest rate in 2007 in response to the reduced liquidity in the interbank money markets (as doubts surfaced following Paribas' refusal in August 2007 to allow withdrawals from mortgage backed securities funds). When the crisis reached storm proportions after Lehman Brothers went down in September 2008, the ECB stepped in November with a single refinancing operation, so that debts in the wholesale bond market could be renewed and extended. As the central banker to Europe's commercial banks, it was legally obliged to accommodate the banks' need for liquidity. What the ECB was not permitted to do was to address the insolvency of banks. Lehman Brothers' failure had an electrifying effect on the US federal authorities, bringing the insolvency issue to the forefront. As explained below (Banking Union section), Europe is only now implementing wide-ranging reforms to resolve a future banking crisis.

The initial view in the European Commission was that the GFC was a US centred problem and that Europe's banks operated according to higher standards of behaviour. This turned out to be wishful thinking. The craziness of sub-prime mortgages was a US phenomenon, but the sale of those impaired and worthless derivatives affected all international banks. Two Bavarian banks (Hypo and Vereins Banken) eventually failed. Commerzbank had to be bailed out, after its mortgage subsidiary the Hypo bank went under. The Dresdner bank failed and was merged with Commerzbank. Deutsche Bank was notorious for selling on their collateral debt obligations to unsuspecting German Landesbanks. Had the US Treasury not saved AIG, which insured the bad trades of the investment banks, then Deutsche Bank and Credit Lyonnais would have probably failed.

In Europe, the financial crisis was seen as a national problem not a pan-European problem, though in fact it was a global problem requiring international solutions. This of course reflected the constitutional position that banking supervision came under national jurisdiction. But rescuing (what were international) banks on a national basis was extremely expensive in *political* capital. In 2009 an incredulous German Chancellor was forced to go to the Bundestag for a €500 billion bailout for Germany's supposedly safe banks. The parliamentarians were being asked to divert fiscal expenditure into the banking system and to underwrite credits backed up with citizen taxation. The Bundesbank under Maastricht rules, just like any other national central bank, was not allowed to undertake the classic Bagehotian monetization of bad banking debt. France was in exactly the same situation and suffered equal political obloquy from its citizens when bail-out measures were put through.

The same French and German banks had been recycling the saving and profit surpluses of northern Europe's economy to the peripheries of Europe, and as noted in Chapter 5, much of this investment was speculative and in certain countries corrupt. However, finance ministries in Greece, Spain, Portugal and Ireland did not have the resources to divert expenditure into their bankrupt banks. Their economic activity plummeted with the withdrawal of credit, and the complete mistrust of counterparty risk. Taxation revenue fell, leading inevitably to the inability of national exchequers to service their debt obligations, and making further loans from the bond markets extremely expensive.

6.1 The European Financial Stability Fund

At this point – 2011 – the single European market and monetary union were facing disintegration. The remedy was the European Financial Stability Fund (EFSF) as a bail-out facility. All EZ national Parliaments were asked to put aside expenditures into a European fund (initially €750 billion) and each country was liable for this new lending in proportion to its GDP. The event was historic. A fund had, at last, been created and all EZ governments had agreed to it. Under duress a joint responsibility was accepted. This liability was specifically particularised to each country which serviced the debt at its ongoing rate of interest, and this meant that countries with less solvent budgets paid a higher charge on the debt. So, this was a form a qualified solidarity. Again, the European *Central* Bank was legally prevented from issuing a common loan, since state and bank bail-outs were outlawed. Instead the executive decisions of the heads of state had brought into existence (in an emergency meeting in May 2010) the EFSF, as a temporary measure.

But at the level of national electorates, the politics turned sour. Each nation's taxpayers were being turned against each other's. For example, Spanish taxpayers were quite aware that their contribution was regressive, the poorer the nation the greater the cost; also, that Berlin and Paris had ordained that the excessive private banks loans of northern banks should be repaid close to 100 cents on the Euro.[3] The weakest countries were subject to the most expensive re-financing packages. And German citizens were again being asked for a large contribution, this time to re-finance southern European countries whose labour costs were higher than the average German worker. Since the Social Democrats' 'Harz' reforms of 2004, Germany has cut its labour costs to pursue export markets.[4] Higher domestic consumption and shorter working hours were foregone, and this turned out to have a seriously de-stabilizing effect on the European economy.[5] We return to this in Chapter 7.

Brussels missed the 'Hamiltonian moment' presented by the crisis to instigate genuine federal solutions. Simeon Djankov, the finance minister of Bulgaria had an insider's seat, as a member of Ecofin, from 2009 to 2014. (Unlike the other insider account provided by the finance minister of Greece in 2015, Yanis Varoufakis, Djankov came from the World Bank and operated with a micro-economic theory that stressed the need for the profitability of business and a balanced budget on the part of government.) At the Commission, Djankov notes, President Barroso did nothing, and Juncker as head of the Ecofin group repeated the mantra of Delors, Kohl et al that a federal solution would be found. Djankov explains that this was not forthcoming because Commissioners were nominated by national governments and it was happenstance whether a Commissioner with financial experience was nominated. 'This lack of initiative [from Brussels] had developed historically from overdependence on the largest member states, mostly Germany. [...] Neither President Barroso nor President Herman Van Rompuy nor Commissioner Rehn were empowered to propose a plan.'[6]

The incident at Deauville in 2010 illustrates the way in which the imperative for executive action concentrated leadership not only in the hands of Germany and France, but their leaders – in private conversation (in a restaurant). Merkel and Sarkozy announced that the European Financial Stability Fund should henceforth involve private sector participation, which was taken to mean that the banks would have to take a 'hair-cut' on their bad loans. This produced a favourable reaction in public opinion and signalled an attempted return to individual financial responsibility of banks. But the macro consequences were not happy. The bond markets took it as a sign that they would not be re-paid on their extensive lines of credit to banks, and they duly raised their interest rates at a time when the solvency of banks (and states) was still grievously fragile. The banking system was in intensive care, not walking on its own two feet. The public responsibility of politicians was the restoration of confidence in the overall banking system. The year before the US Treasury Secretary Timothy Geithner, invited to an Ecofin meeting, had said as much. 'Geithner's chief recommendation was that the European Central Bank should *somehow* signal its readiness to underwrite the debt of key countries, such as Italy, to show that Europe was prepared to stop the domino effect threatening the eurozone.'[7] His advice was angrily rejected by national finance ministers. The emphasis on 'somehow' is ours. The ECB could not escape its no-monetization clause of banks or state debt.

What had alarmed Geithner during his visit to Europe was the Ecofin's totally unforgiving attitude to Greece's problems. Greece had few allies in northern and eastern European countries; clientalism, corruption, mendacity all of which had ballooned out its state and private debts. It was no longer a trusted political counterparty. However, it was in a doom loop of bankrupt banks, a bankrupt Treasury, and the disintegration of the Greek state. Though a very minor economy, its fall would have had a domino effect on weaker Eurozone economies. Geithner commented: 'You can put your foot on the neck of those guys if that's what you want to do. But you've got to make sure you send a countervailing signal of reassurance to Europe and the world that you are going to hold things together and not let it go.'[8]

The reassurance that went out was that all those periphery countries that had excessive state and banking debts would be subject to enforced austerity progammes. Putting aside the highly controversial question of whether austerity cures or intensifies the problem – essentially a matter of competing economists' paradigms – what was the political form of this rectification package?

The package consisted of two aspects, a bailout fund, which was replacing the (unpopular) EFSF and the imposition of austerity: reduction in labour costs and the cost of pensions, tax harmonisation, and fiscal discipline keeping budget deficits within a prescribed limit.[9] The fund was again subscribed to on a per EZ nation basis and this amounted overall to two thirds of the fund, and the other third was provided by the IMF. This was a highly political decision. Chancellor Merkel only agreed to the IMF's involvement as a way of appeasing her voters, particularly aggrieved by a *second* bailout call that had to be approved by the Bundestag. From an international, especially southern hemisphere perspective, this was seen as a misuse of IMF funds. Europe was surely wealthy enough to sort its own problems out, was the view. From a prestige point of view it was a European humiliation. It was perpetrated because politically Chancellor Merkel wanted it done that way. Germany did not want to be seen as imposing austerity, even though this was its established position in relation to EZ rules. But from a pan-European perspective it was a very retrograde step. The IMF bails out sovereign states and so the rescue mission was viewed through a national, country-specific prism. Europe was abdicating its responsibility to resolve its problems as a federal entity.

The administration of the EFSF remains its most controversial feature. Control over the fund was shared by the

ECB, the IMF, and the European Commission. As the largest contributor to the fund, Berlin had a decisive influence. The troika was an authoritarian form of executive power, whose legacy may well have already laid the fracture between northern EZ countries (Germany, Netherlands, Benelux and Finland) and southern countries (Greece, Portugal, Spain as well as Ireland). N.b. Italy was not on the list. Funds would be transferred to sovereign but technically bankrupt Treasuries as long as they carried out the prescribed austerity programme and a schedule of loan repayments, which were administered directly by German and IMF officials. The short term economic logic of this programme was irrational, for with a collapse of government expenditure, wages, and capital outflow, these economies shrank – in Greece's case by some 25%.[10] The repayment of loans to the troika and the ESFC became near impossible, and led to fantastical arrangements in the Greek case.[11]

The logic of enforced austerity was more political than economic. Varoufakis argues that his nation had to be crushed in order to point the way to other deficit countries – *pour encourager les autres* to quote Voltaire. The economic justifications of austerity were rather a cover for a transformation of polities, termed by the troika as structural adjustment. Campbell and Hall have persuasively argued that peripheral states like Ireland and Greece suffered from longstanding weak state infrastructure, regulatory weakness and clientalism at the level of both the interests of capital and labour. This was particularly marked, indeed spectacularly so, in the banking, real estate and construction sectors, a commonality in Greece, Ireland, Spain and Portugal. In this sense enforcing structural change to the organization of the state itself was well overdue, something Varoufakis himself acknowledges.[12] But the political damage, for the countries affected, was massive. Governments in Spain, Italy and France decided it was better to introduce austerity measures themselves, so avoiding the degradation of asking for EFSF relief. Portugal also introduced austerity measures but was forced by speculative pressure in the bond markets to apply to the troika in May 2011 for a bailout. This meant that a common resistance to austerity measures by those countries was muted.

Electorates were not muted in their anger. Bailouts were recycled through the insolvent Greek banks to repay loans to German and French banks, just as austerity savings were used to pay back foreign bank loans. Governments fell and popular protest movements sprang up – on the ground as well as making significant inroads into national parliaments. Recession, anger with corruption in government and banking, and huge spikes in unemployment led to the fall of the Spanish Socialist Workers Party in 2011, likewise in the same year the Portuguese Socialist Party. In Eire the Fianna Fáil governing party fell to fourth place in opinion polls after the Taoiseach announced the country was asking for a large loan from the troika, and it was defeated in the 2011 election. In Greece the Prime Minister, Papandreou, resigned in 2011 in the face of the troika bailout and its conditionality. His ruling party PASOK, now in coalition with the right wing New Democracy, was decimated in the 2012 elections, with New Democracy just hanging on as the centre parties imploded.

The political fall-out was not one-sided. The True Finns made an electoral break-through in March 2011, Marine le Pen had free ammunition for her anti-Euro populist cause, and in Germany the Alternativen für Deutschland were founded in 2013. The bilateralism of paying in accentuated political differences between member countries, leading to a permanent diminution of European solidarity. In the UK there was palpable relief that it had not entered the Euro, lending support to anti-EU sentiment.

The EFSF was an emergency device and the political decision making behind it was driven by crisis. It had no legal status under EU Treaties. However, its substantive nature – bailouts conditional upon austerity and structural adjustment – remained in place in its successor organization, the European Stability Mechanism (ESM). This was given legal status by a two-line amendment, by the European Commission, of Article 137 of TFEU. This was approved by the European Parliament in March 2011, as follows: 'The member states whose currency is the euro may establish a stability mechanism to be activated if indispensable to safeguard the stability of the euro area as a whole. The granting of any required financial assistance under the mechanism will be made subject to strict conditionality.'

This illustrates well the way in which exigency forced a solution that was quasi-federal and executive in nature and its acquisition of *legal* legitimacy. The ESM is being further developed into a European Monetary Fund. This brings us back to the starting point of the European monetary project. ESM is a fund of €80 billion with all EZ members paying in in proportion to their GDP, making Germany, France, Italy and Spain the main contributors. The ESM has the capacity to increase this support to a €500 billion lending capacity. Therefore the EZ is now putting in place a fund, which the original planners thought essential. That noted, the two EMFs differ substantially in their operation. The ESM has rigid conditionality, the Fiscal Compact, which controversially enforces deficit rules on national finance departments and those conditions are subject to the European Court of Justice. National sovereignty is ceded to the board of governors of the ESM, who are placed beyond any parliamentary control. Also, the extra lending facility is delivered by going to the private capital markets, and not creating credit intrinsic to the fund (as was the case with bancor in the original IMF design or the IMF's later special drawing rights).

6.2 Banking Unions and Reactions to the GFC

The general theme in this report is a comparison between the Federal Reserve of the United States with the more recently arrived European Central Bank (ECB). Both institutions have played functional roles in the development of federal governmental structures in the USA and in the European Union. As previously discussed both play a role in political structures that continues to evolve. This section highlights the element of evolutionary change of both the Fed and the ECB with respect to banking reforms.

Table 4.4 in chapter 4 shows that both the US and the EU expended more than 20% of their respective GDPs in 'unconventional' monetary policies to effect a long drawn out turn-around in their economies. The GFC was a banking crisis, so one of the first acts of a politically sensible polity is to institute banking reforms and make supervision of banks more rigorous. Roosevelt's Emergency Banking Act went through both Houses of Congress in eight hours and was approved by the President that same evening. The Act forced the closure of all banks in the US for a week and enforced mergers and closures that reduced the overall number of banks in the US from 17,300 to 10,000 thousand banks in 1933.[13] In the US the legislators passed the Dodds-Frank Act in 2010 and the EU agreed the Banking Union in December 2014. Once again the United States was quicker off the mark, but the implementation process in both has faced major problems. The Dodds-Frank Act was deemed too complex and its implementation was slowed down, to this day, by vigorous lobbying on Capitol Hill. The European Banking Union indicates the lack of speedy political responsiveness, and its implementation reveals a fundamental argument about whether the reforms operate at federal level or belong to national jurisdictions.

President Roosevelt and his economic advisors bypassed the Federal Reserve in reforming the banking system, and it was only in 1935 under the chairmanship of Marriner Eccles that the Federal Reserve assumed new powers consonant with the New Deal reform programme. A government agency, the Federal Reconstruction Corporation re-capitalized the banks, and it (not the Fed) instituted a Federal Bank Deposit Insurance (FDIC) scheme. For banks to be included in the deposit insurance they had to submit to oversight of their balance sheet, loan book and remuneration of employees and owners. All of the major banks were obliged to become members of the Federal Reserve System. Roosevelt had a democratic mandate to reform the private and joint stock banks, very much bolstered by the hearings of the Senate Banking and Currency Committee (with Ferdinand Pecora as counsel) into the malfeasance, insider deals and commercial insanity of the banks. New and old legislation was used to enact these measures, speedily. A new federal executive had emerged in response to the exigency of economic crisis and the demands of an angry electorate.

The important points to watch here are that the US federal government, and its main economic agency, the federal Treasury, were able to institute US wide reforms and changes that were applied relatively uniformly across the entire federation. There were no exceptions, opt outs or other examples of foot dragging. The circumstances were sufficiently serious to book little interference. The perceived alternative to the proposed course of action was further chaos and disintegration.

The institutions established at that time, which included a federation wide banking union largely run by the FDIC, guaranteed that small depositors would not be wiped out in case of another slump, thus restoring confidence at a crucial time. The strength of the institutions launched were to prove sufficiently strong that they lasted until the next GFC in 2008. At which point a number of serious weaknesses and shortcomings were identified. In the US this meant that there was a clear functional responsibility already in place identifying who would be responsible for clearing up the ensuing mess.

However, there had been some important changes in the world since the 1930s, and these had in many respects passed by the regulatory framework established then. While clearly a continental federation, the linkages with the rest of the world in the financial sector had clearly multiplied and deepened. The impact of the US based crisis in the residential property sector spread rapidly to complex financial products in Wall Street, and from there across to Europe and the rest of the world. One of the last customers for a portfolio of CDOs sold by Lehman Brothers, literally seconds before it ceased trading, was to a German Landesbank which was effectively guaranteed by the German government.

6.3 US Reactions to the GFC

As the 'originator' of the crisis, US authorities reacted relatively quickly. The GFC came at an awkward time, just as the presidential baton was being handed over from President Bush to Obama, and during the middle of a Presidential election campaign.

The reaction immediately involved several areas of the federal government. These included the President, the US Congress, the Federal Reserve, and other federal institutions. While these institutions did not necessarily all work in the same direction, or sing off the same hymn sheet, there was a degree of cross-party recognition that the severity of the situation required some dramatic forms of assistance to prevent a repeat of the 1930s. And in many respect this was achieved.

The initial TARP programme, a Treasury programme of US$ 700 billions of aid to the financial and non-financial sectors was rapidly approved by Congress. And this money was disbursed rapidly. It can partly be seen as a financial fix, as well as containing elements of a fiscal injection of funds. The banking and insurance industries were major recipients of assistance, and these funds went largely to recapitalize the banks. Large portions of the automobile industry were bailed out, including the rescue of General Motors, previously a bell weather of the US economy, and Chrysler, that was then sold to Fiat. Other sectors also benefited.

There were some notable casualties amongst Federal financial institutions, including Freddie Mac and Fannie Mae, two institutions lying deep at the heart of the property mortgage system that had become overwhelmed by claims and were effectively bankrupt. Several large commercial banks were put into special measures including Citibank, by some measures the largest bank in the world with a truly global presence. A number of large regional banks and some savings and loans institutions went under as well, requiring infusions of liquidity. Unlike the early stages of the Great Depression lessons had been learned. Bernanke, the chairman of the Federal Reserve exercised a calming influence and ensured that liquidity was available if needed.

The Fed fully played up to its role of lender of last resort.

Nevertheless, it was clear that there were some major weaknesses in the federal union of the United States. A whole layer of non-banking financial institutions had effectively avoided more onerous banking regulations, and no financial regulator either formally had responsibility for monitoring them, nor had a responsibility for dealing with bankruptcies and liquidations.

In 2009, with the crisis still unfolding, the President began initial soundings for broader reforms of the banking system. This time there was no question of avoiding the Federal Reserve, it was involved from the start. By 2010 under the leadership of Senator Dodd and Congressman Frank, legislation was introduced into both chambers of the legislature to expedite the introduction of the most serious reform of the banking system since the 1930s. The equivalent for the EU/EZ would have been the simultaneous introduction of legislative changes to the Council of Minister (Senate equivalent) and the European Parliament (House of Representatives equivalent.). This did not happen in Europe.

The Dodd-Frank Act entitled the Wall Street Reform and Consumer Protection Act was passed on July 21 2010, at a time when many in the EZ were not yet fully convinced there was a major storm brewing.

Dodd-Frank Act. Summary View

The Act has some 6 main components. For the sake of improving understanding of what happened in the EU, and in particular the development of a Banking Union, it is worth mentioning that the US already has a Banking Union. However, as the GFC showed, having a banking union on its own is insufficient to protect against systemic risks that build up in financial systems.

The US legislature, not the Fed, took the opportunity to make a series of important legal and procedural changes, designed in the main to once again prevent the repeat of the GFC, and to do this by trying to change behaviour. As in the 1930s, there are clear signs of the stable door once more being shut long after the horse has bolted.

The Act sought to make changes in the following areas:

1. There was a consolidation of regulatory agencies, the abolition of some, and the creation of others. An oversight council was established to specifically evaluate systemic risks. Little has been heard of Financial Stability Council since.
2. There was a general tightening up of regulations, and the introduction of regulations in areas previously free from them. This includes rules on derivative trading – they have to be traded on formal exchanges, and rules on financial advisors working with hedge funds.
3. There are new consumer protection rules, including a higher level of deposit insurance, and increased investor protection.
4. A new resolution procedure was set up to deal with the orderly winding up of banks and other institutions facing liquidity crises. This has resulted in a new Resolution procedure for systemically important banks, which complements and expands earlier procedures organized by the FDIC. Importantly this includes a dispensation from the Treasury to the Fed to extend additional loans in 'unusual or exigent circumstances'.
5. There are tighter rules for credit rating institutions.
6. And finally, a Volcker rule was introduced for banks and non-banks preventing own account, or 'nostro' account proprietary trading.

These measures enjoyed support across a wide range of federal institutions initially, but the complexity of the Act has created its own problems. The Act with addenda is thousands of pages, whereas the 1933 Glass-Steagall Act was a mere 37 pages. There are 14 different titles, or parts of the Dodd-Frank reforms. Not all of them are handled in a single piece of legislation, and some have been introduced separately.

Two new institutions were established, the Financial Stability Oversight Council (FSOC), and the Office of Financial Research (OFR). The OFR bears a similarity to the Office of Budget Responsibility (OBR) in the UK. The FSOC and the OFR are designed to work closely together. The FSOC has ten voting members, all of whom have federal regulatory experience. The tenth member is the chairperson, the Secretary of the Treasury, a role that does not exist in the EZ/EU. There are also 5 non-voting supporting members with sector expertise.

One of the important roles of the FSOC is to define and monitor large financial institutions that have assets of more than US$ 50 billion. These are defined as Systemically Important Financial Institutions (SIFI), and they can be specifically monitored and controlled by the FSOC. This would appear to make some inroads on the Fed's role in managing the US banking union. The Office of Financial Research (OFR) is located in the Treasury department. Its head is chosen by the President, and approved by the Senate.[14]

The FSOC meets quarterly and reports to Congress. It is tasked with identifying threats to the financial stability of the USA. It has to promote market discipline, and it should respond to emerging threats. Since its formation it has not gained a great deal of external publicity. The FSOC also has powers, when there is a two thirds majority, to include foreign banks in the SIFI group, and it can order special reports/audits on SIFI institutions if needed.

This enforcement role is backed by the OFR, who has the power to issue subpoenas from any bank or financial institution, and can contribute analysis to the FSOC enforcement actions.

Orderly liquidation

The GFC revealed how difficult and complex it was to wind up large banks and non-banking financial institutions. The winding up orders either had to be made through normal bankruptcy procedures and through the usual court processes. The FDIC and the Securities Investor Protection Corporation could also initiate proceedings.

The Dodd-Frank Act has shifted the responsibility of this to the FSOC, and also extended the range of these orderly liquidation to include insurance companies. Previously this had been handled by the Federal Insurance Office, part of the US Treasury.

It also looks as if the FSOC will be infringing on Fed responsibilities in other areas too. In the past responsibility of general liquidations was handled by the FDIC or the Fed; Broker/Dealer bankruptcies by either the SEC or the Fed. It now appears that for the larger 'too big to fail' banks, their liquidity issues will be dealt with by the FSOC. And the other organization mainly responsibility for financial sector liquidations remains with the FDIC. [15]

A further innovation is the introduction of an Orderly Liquidation fund. This is to be slowly capitalized over a period no less than 5 and no more than 10 years. Banks and financial institutions with assets of more than US$ 50 billion will be asked to contribute to this fund. Their contributions will be a function of the extent and nature of their risk weighted assets. Even so, the government is limiting its obligations for orderly liquidation to a value of either 10% of the assets, or to 90% of the fair value of any remaining assets. So this is far from being a large, comprehensive bailout.

There are many other elements of the Dodd-Frank Act that are too numerous to be mentioned here. The general tenor is to tighten up on regulation, and extend regulation to credit agencies, hedge fund advisors, swaps and derivatives. More uniform standards are being introduced across a range of financial products and a number of additional regulatory bodies are being established.

While the Dodd-Frank Act offers a comprehensive view, its implementation and success remain under scrutiny. Paul Volcker was dubious (writing in 2013): 'As to whether the system as a whole has become more stable, one should ponder on the view that the current boom in equities is closely related to the abnormally low level of fixed income bond yields. And this is one product of the QE policies being run by both the Fed and the ECB.' Volcker thought it had 'implicitly recognized and even reinforced the range of Federal Reserve regulatory and supervisory authority', though noting that the vice chairman of the supervisory board was unfilled it left open the question 'whether the administration and the Federal Reserve really appreciate the long-term significance of maintaining the Fed's supervisory responsibilities.' Complexity remains a weakness: 'following Dodd-Frank, we are left with a half-dozen distinct regulatory agencies involved in banking and finance, each with its own mandate, its own institutional loyalties and support networks in Congress, along with an ever-growing cadre of lobbyists equipped with the capacity to provide campaign financing.'[16]

6.4 EZ and EU Banking Union and reaction to the GFC

The Single Rulebook, promulgated via the European Banking Authority (EBA) has introduced a series of financial regulations and directives which apply *to all 28 EU members*. These include the Capital Requirements Directive and the Capital Requirements Regulation; the Bank Recovery and Resolution Directive, and the Deposit Guarantee Scheme Directive. These lay down capital requirements for banks; create regulations covering the prevention and management of bank failures, and establish a minimum level of protection for depositors. There is also a European Systemic Risk Board (ESRB) which is responsible for macro-prudential oversight.

The Single Rulebook was a recommendation/directive of the European Council made in June 2009 and intended as a continuation of the legislation of the Single Market across the whole of the European Union. Its key objectives were: (1) eliminate legislative differences among member states, (2) ensure the same level of protection for consumers, (3) ensure a level playing field for all banks across the EU. The intention therefore was to iron out national differences and to create a common standard at the federal level.

In looking at the detail of these proposals, two points emerge. Their actual legislation will be drawn out over a period of time, and the process of that legislation in certain areas is disputed. In particular, there is a major argument about their federal/universal application or their particularization to national jurisdictions.

The Banking Union is compulsory for all EZ members, and is optional for other EU member states. The creation of the Banking Union in the EU has to be approved by all of the EUs member states, not just the EZ members. The European Parliament went on to approve the Banking Union on the

16 December 2014, meaning that the Banking Union came into *partial* operation in 2015. There is a transitional period lasting until 2025 by which time all the relevant members must have completed and implemented the legal changes.

The Banking Union has three pillars:

1. The Single Supervisory Mechanism (SSM) under which the ECB is the main, central supervisory authority across the EZ, performing its supervisory tasks in cooperation with the National Regulators. This mechanism has been agreed and is operational. The SSM was approved by the EP in October 2013 (1022/2013). The ECB will take direct oversight of the 128 banks and financial institutions (lenders) held to be systemically important for financial stability. These will now be monitored by the Federal ECB and not by national central banks. The ECB will also take on additional supervisory powers for an additional 6,600 banks that are large, but not systemically important, and who are currently supervised by national central bank.

2. The Single Resolution Mechanism (SRM), comprising the Single Resolution Board (SRB) and the National Regulators of the banking union countries, with access to the Single Resolution Fund (SRF), financed via an Intergovernmental Agreement which arranges and mutualizes the national contributions to the SRF. Each country is to create a Resolution Fund, and it will be capitalized over an 8-year period. The Single Resolution Mechanism (EU 1093/2010) started on 1 January 2016, and will continue until 2024. The aim is to build up a fund of €55 billion. The Resolution fund differs from the depositor insurance fund, since these funds are pooled and are not allocated on a national basis, even though every member state has to have one. This applies to the whole of the EU, and not just to the EZ. Non-member states can also apply, suggesting

that a post Brexit UK could also become involved in this scheme. So far it has been used once to enable the takeover of Banco Popular by Banco Santander in Spain. (N.b. Banco Popular was a small bank, not posing any substantial systemic risk).

There is another important innovation. For the first time investors in banks will be 'bailed in' to any rescue and restructuring measures. The aim is to ensure that private investors, particularly bank bond holders who were previously exempt from contributing to restructuring costs, will now be expected to bear some of the losses if a bank is forced into liquidation. This is covered by the Bank Recovery and Resolution Directive. It became operational as of 2015 and is limited to up to 8% of a bank's liabilities. It will also apply to non-members of the Banking Union.

3. The European Deposit Insurance Scheme (EDIS) which will provide a mutual insurance fund at EZ / Banking Union level. This will be funded by a bank depositor insurance fund, similar to the US FDIC. These funds will be built up by banks to the sum of €44 billion. This will be built up slowly for ten years after 2015. Importantly, these funds are designated as belonging to each member state. It is unclear on what basis these funds will be collected. This scheme has *not* been agreed and is the subject of strong objections from Germany, Netherlands, Finland, and Austria.

These political objections rest on attitudes towards risk in terms of non-performing loans on the books of some southern European countries, e.g. Italy. The deeper sources of these objections are the major structural economic problem (which we have discussed elsewhere) of the difference between the export-oriented northern European countries, i.e. notably Germany, and the southern European consumer demand-led countries (one might also here include the UK).

So, from one perspective the Banking Union would seem to involve a significant transfer of power to the EU federal level, driven – even though belatedly – by the exigencies of bank failure, loose and inadequate supervision, and the demand that European citizens be afforded a degree of protection. But the political objections contain in themselves a different perspective on federalism and how risk and responsibility should be allocated.

Dr Schäuble articulates very well this second perspective. Wolfgang Schäuble until late 2017 was Germany's Finance Minister and was the longest serving member of Ecofin. His voice was by far the most influential in the Eurogroup. While an initial champion of banking union, he said that the reforms required, in addition, treaty changes. 'Banking union only makes sense ... if we also have rules for restructuring and resolving banks. But if we want European institutions for that, we will need a treaty change.' And in another statement Dr Schäuble said, 'You can do the same thing very well with a network of national authorities.'[17] At a substantive level Germany did not want its domestic banking system at regional and local level subject to a European supervisory board. The argument is not without merit. The ecology of German banks owes much to mutual saving schemes and the network of re-capitalization of the banks postwar by the Kredit für Wiederaufbau corporation. Like Italy the local banks are rooted in, including ownership, small and medium enterprises. It is also doubtful whether adequate supervisory expertise – always a fallible métier – exists in Frankfurt and the ECB.

Generalizing Schäuble's position, rules embedded in treaties represent the federal level of executive action. Implementation belongs and is owned by each member state. The same formulation applies to the Fiscal Compact as well as any movement towards Fiscal Union, where all states will operate under the same budget rules – an echo of eighteenth century German cameralism. Everyone works to the same set of rules, and diversity in application or interpretation is not allowed. The federal vision is akin to everyone living in identical houses, ordered from above. Putting it more starkly, each member country proceeds as a clone of German arrangements.

In fact 'German arrangements' have had considerable flexibility in Germany itself in its postwar history as federal political republic. What is referred to is Ordoliberalism, which Chancellor Merkel supports. In an address at the Walter Eucken Institute in 2016, she declared that 'the Ordo-liberal principles of the Freiburg School have lost nothing in currency and importance.' The state institutes the legal rules within which free markets operate. The prohibition against monetizing state or bank debt, fundamental to the attitude of the Bundesbank, comes directly from Ordoliberalism; as does intolerance of fiscal discretion by government which, of course, was Keynes' prescription for escaping a liquidity trap; likewise as Marriner Eccles noted, it was not possible to extricate a national economy from depression by 'pushing on a piece of string'.

Ordoliberalism has a more precise notion of moral hazard. Mutualization of debt, whether the debt of banks or states, affronts the principle of *Haftung*. All economic agents are liable, that is responsible for their debts. Andreas Kluth, in explaining Haftung in *Handelsblatt*, says this is why Germans oppose a common European deposit insurance. 'It could mean that Germans pay for a failed bank in Italy, rather as Texans in theory might have to vouch for Californian depositors.'[18] But, of course, since 1935 Texans have not had to do this, because the US has had a Federal Deposit scheme. Equally, irresponsible real estate speculation in Florida, does not condemn that state to fiscal and commercial strangulation. US citizens have every right to complain about the terms on which the mega banks were bailed out in 2008, but they don't do this as Texans or Californians.

6.5 Banking Union Conclusions

Going into the GFC the US had an operating banking union, while the EU did not. The existence of a banking union did not prevent the GFC in the US. It may well have made it easier, and quicker, to clear up the debris afterwards.

The EU/EZ has had to acquire a banking union, and make it work, as a sine qua non for having an operational and secure banking system. After all, the minimum critical function banks have to perform is to look after their clients' money, and in some respects this they signally failed to do. The fact that the damage did not extend to multiple bank failures was entirely due to the ex gratia payments made by the tax payers at the behest of their national governments. There was no generalized Resolution process in place that could be applied to large, multination, meso level banks and banking authorities.

The most dramatic holes in the banking security system are now being plugged. For the time being it is to be hoped that the core of the EU banking system is fit for purpose. This does not mean that all the fires have been extinguished. Problems persist in Greece and Italy, and the system remains fragile. Clearly there was no federal set of institutions in place when the GFC broke, and there is no doubt a confederal basis for banking supervision failed. The coordination and trust problems between national supervisors slowed down and complicated the recovery process. That said, the emergent model of banking supervision is federal in character. The crisis has shown that the EU commission, the Council of Ministers, the ECB and the European Parliament have managed to put forward and legislate on a new modified and revised structure that will help to prevent future crises. Against that, German influence over the Banking Union stands in direct conflict with the latter's key objectives as formulated by the European Commission. This is considered further in the next chapter.

6.6 The ECB discovers its central purpose

The ECB finally stepped up to the plate in March 2012 with the credit easing of €530 billion to 800 banks *across* the EZ, so saving the whole Euro credit system from collapse. It also bought 'marketable' assets from Greek banks – an operation it repeated again in July prior to Greek elections. In August 2012 the ECB offered to buy the government bonds of those countries faced with dual bankruptcy. In this way, by driving down interest rates to lower levels, it sidelined the facilities of the ESM, which were no longer requested (except by Cyprus). The ECB had graduated to the status of a true central bank, effectively acting as a lender of last resort.

But an important complication has to be noted. The Federal Reserve, or the Bank of England, comes to the aid of the banking system across the whole of the country. This is not feasible in the European confederation, where this is the responsibility of each country's central bank. But in the formation of the ECB a major part of those reserves was moved to the ECB. And, to repeat, by EU Treaty the ECB cannot monetize state debt. So, just how does the ECB provide relief for embattled state treasuries and their banks? Mario Draghi the new chairman of the ECB executive announced in mid 2012, 'Within our mandate the ECB is prepared to do whatever it takes to preserve the Euro.' So how did he deliver the promise of unlimited liquidity?

Yanis Varoufakis describes the operation. Greece had been forced into the troika regime, and the prime ministers of Italy and Spain, Mario Monti and Mariano Rajoy, saw their tenure under threat from a similar fate. Instead they 'would not have to borrow from other European taxpayers: their debt would be bolstered by money printed by the ECB'.[19] This was the Outright Monetary Transaction, where at a time of its choosing, the ECB would step into the market to buy unlimited quantities of Italian and Spanish bonds. Draghi defended this policy as maintaining the clause in its charter that it should maintain full control over the interest rates that businesses and households paid. The bond markets, at the time, were experiencing raging volatility, hence the ECB needed to provide the guiding hand. The OMT never had to be actuated, trust had returned to the bond market and as an analyst later commented: 'The ECB's evolution to lender of last resort has blunted market pressure and political momentum'.[20]

A year later the ECB embarked upon quantitative easing, as the permanent means of keeping interest rates low. €60 billion a month was to be expended on this, the money being created on the balance sheet of the ECB, as was the case with the Federal Reserve, the Bank of England and the Bank of Japan. The ECB, again adhering to the maxim of ensuring effective monetary conditions, bought a country's bonds irrespective whether their finances were sound or in difficulty.

Hence German bonds were bought, in proportion to GDP, driving down already low interest rates. In central bank theory, the ECB should buy only distressed assets. And it should only do this on a temporary basis, leaving governments and business to restore the economy to better health. Businesses however receive a windfall advantage from cheap credit, and the evidence shows that when profitability was re-established those profits were used for unproductive share buy-backs, and mergers and acquisitions – none of which boosted the real economy but instead encouraged rentier behaviour.

The ECB was gradually evolving into a proper central bank, but with some perverse arrangements and outcomes. Its actions had become federal in extent, but the executive of the ECB is still bound by the Lisbon Treaty. The change in direction was very much related to Draghi's leadership. And, as we have seen, the ECB has been able to resist the challenge of the Bundesbank. The independence of the ECB from national interests was affirmed, and in acting as a lender of last resort it realized the intrinsic attribute of a central bank and its responsibilities to uphold the federal currency.

6.7 Executive federalism and democratic legitimacy

The measures taken up in the scramble to deal with the GFC, as it impacted Europe, mark a sharp rise in executive federalism in Ecofin, the Eurogroup, the Stability Fund, and the ECB. The Eurogroup was very much the coordinating and enforcing agency. Its membership was predominantly finance ministers working with the European Commission, the ECB and with the IMF, so making it the executive committee of the troika. Its thinking and decisions fed directly into the Ecofin meetings whose decisions were affirmed by Council.

The Eurogroup can claim legal legitimacy, for as an EZ inter-governmental body, it is recognised by the TFEU in respect of voting rights over Eurozone issues. Accordingly Protocol 14 of the Lisbon Treaty dealing with the Eurogroup, indicates that the main task of the Eurogroup is 'to discuss questions related to the specific responsibilities they [the ministers of Eurozone Member States] share with regard to the single currency'. But it has no specific legal authority as a federal or confederal body to make far-reaching decision. This constitutional vagueness about the position of the Euro-group (which is currently at odds in the context of the EU as a 'community of laws') means that there is neither account-ability to any EU institution, e.g. the European Parliament, nor any transparency, i.e. there is no available minute of meetings of discussions.

In acting as the fiscal 'government' of the EZ, the Euro-group has exercised considerable discretionary power. This may be viewed as attempting – with some success – *to impose a federal structure of its own making on the Eurozone*. Its creation and enforcement of the Fiscal Compact is particu-larly controversial. This has prevented individual countries from using fiscal policy to reflate their economies. In repre-sentative party democracy these draconian measures would have to be defended and justified and approved by a majority. The European Parliament, which is a representative assembly with well-defined political parties, was given no such oppor-tunity. The Eurogroup was not necessarily wrong in calling for some reductions in budget deficits at certain points in the crisis, for when they did bond markets were stabilized. But parliamentary, that is legislative approval, has historically been shown to be equally forceful. Also, through parlia-mentary select committees, policies can be improved, which was certainly feasible in the face of the *pauschal*, one-size-fits-all austerity of the Eurogroup.

Notes

1. Harold James, *Making the European Monetary Union* (Harvard University Press, 2012), pp. 212-14.

2. Chares Calomiris and Stephen Haber, *Fragile by Design. The Political Origins of Banking Crises and Scarce Credit* (Princeton University Press, 2014), pp. 203-6.

3. This is analysed acerbically in Yanis Varoufakis, *And the Weak Suffer What They Must* (Vintage, 2016), pp. 164-9.

4. There was a certain path dependency to the Harz reforms, since Germany was carrying a greatly increased set of social and rebuilding programmes following on from the absorption of the German Democratic Republic into the Federal Republic. Saving the monetary union, which was still in Germany's best economic interest, was widely perceived as an additional tax burden.

5. From 2004 German wage level increases were consistently below other EU countries, so that average nominal unit labour cost were one of the lowest by 2011 (Djankov, p. 39). Claus Offe recently commented (October 2017) that Germany was a country 'where the lowest 40 per cent of earners have seen no real pay increases in two decades, where every sixth child lives in near-poverty and where no less than 1.5m are being served by food banks' (https://www.socialeurope.eu/germany-happens-next).

6. Simeon Djankov, *Inside the Euro Crisis. An Eyewitness Account* (Peterson Institute for International Economics, 2014), p. 51. Djankov also enters a powerful criticism of the Brussels disregard for the fragile eastern countries not in the EZ, so opening the door to 'the rise of Euroskeptic leaders such as Viktor Orbán in Hungary'.

7. Varoufakis, *And the Weak Suffer*, p. 168.

8. Quoted in Varoufakis, *And the Weak Suffer*, p. 234.

9. Djankov, *Inside*, p. 84.

10. In a shrinking economy the proportion of existing debt to GDP increases. Varoufakis presents a debt to income ratio that shows Ireland going from 25% to 123% from 2008 to 2014, and, for the same period, Portugal going from 68.3% to 129.7%; the figures for Greece are 105.4% to 175%. Varoufakis, *And the Weak Suffer*, p. 291.

11. Yanis Varoufakis, *And the Weak Suffer*, pp. 155-6.

12. John L. Campbell & John A. Hall, *The Paradox of Vulnerabiity. States, Nationalism and the Financial Crisis* (Princeton University Press, 2017). Varoufakis recounts that political elites like Italy and Greece embraced monetary union as way of extending their incompetent tenureship of power until such time as modernization would be imposed from the North, believing that 'Calvinist administrators will take over the nation's reins, turning it into a Germany, or perhaps a Denmark, on the Mediterranean!' (*And the Weak*, p. 109). In fact Denmark was very badly affected by the GFC, not at all Calvinistic. But, as Campbell and Hall show (pp. 45-58), Denmark had a coherently organised state that sprang into action in 2008 to rectify its bank and debt problem. The output foregone by 2011 has been calculated at an awesome 36% of GDP. See IMF Working Paper 12/163 (2012). 'Systemic Banking Crises Database: An Update', L. Laeven and F. Valencia, p. 24

13. Milton Friedman and Anna Schwartz, *A Monetary History of the United States 1867-1960* (Princeton University Press, 1963), pp. 422-425.

14. There was a substantive debate in the UK about whether the OBR should be located inside the Treasury or not. It was decided to be located outside of the Treasury.

15. All of which has a faint echo of the decision by the Labour government to separate banking industry supervision away from the BoE, and towards the then FSA in 1997. A decision that later came to be regretted, since Treasury, the BoE and FSA all went their separate ways.

16. Paul Volcker, 'The Fed and Big Banking at the Crossroads', *New York Review of Books*, August 15, 2013.

17. Quoted in Djankov, pp. 145-6.

18. Andreas Kluth, 'Ordoliberalism and the Alleged Aberrations of German Economics', *Handelsblatt*, January 31 2018.

19. Varoufakis, *And the Weak Suffer*, p. 179.

20. Quoted in Djankov, *Inside the Euro*, p. 134.

Chapter 7
Suggested EZ Reforms

In any governance structure there is a need for demonstrable legitimacy, democratic oversight, and efficient governance procedures. As far as the EZ is concerned none of these three elements is present to a sufficient degree. If the EZ is to not only survive, but also to develop, then these deficient aspects of its structure and operation must be remedied. This chapter attempts to suggest how the resolution of the problem may be approached and examines potential reforms. However, it will be useful first to look at the arguments for a move from confederalism to federalism within the EZ/EU in the light of the early, and continuing, discussions about republican democracy in the USA.

7.1 Federal Democracy: Confederalism to Federalism

In Chapter 6 we indicated the functional socio-economic imperatives arising from GFC but also the democratic limitations of the EZ. However, there are two dimensions of democracy, which in philosophical discussion in the US are not always clarified. A good deal of the discussion in the US stems from the original Jeffersonian Republican versus Hamiltonian Federalist (and later Madison) debates on the US constitution and is concerned with 'republican democracy' in terms of the powers of the federal government vis-à-vis the power of the individual states. There is less discussion about participative democracy involving the populace. We have dealt with the US historical context in Chapter 2, so we will not repeat the discussion here.

Our concern here is about the potential evolution of the current EU mix of federal, confederal, and intergovernmental legal positioning. In some areas of governance the term federal can be applied (the ECB is a supranational institution and has acted in a quasi-federal manner, as we have earlier indicated); in other areas the treaties confer confederal power, e.g. the common commercial policy; in other areas inter-governmental governance obtains, e.g. foreign policy and aid policy.

It is important, therefore, to distinguish the *sui generis* nature of the situation of the EU. We are not dealing with the birth of a nation. The EU comprises an alliance of independent nation-states; some of which are relatively recent constructions, others are much older. Moreover, there is variation in terms of the modes of (and operation of) participative democracy across the EU countries, including the role and relative powers of the state in ensuring the welfare of its citizens. Indeed it is the perception, or misperception, of the 'interference of Brussels' in the daily lives of citizens which fuels antagonism to the EZ/EU and tends to prevent a rational debate on the nature of the current mixed (federal/confederal/intergovernmental) structures of the EU.

It is for these reasons, and the unique nature of the 'federalist' journey embarked on since the inception of the EU, that the lessons to be derived from a comparison with the USA need to be carefully calibrated.

There are clearly similarities in relation to the existence of an EU constitution, a constitutional court (the ECJ), and a directly elected, and powerful parliament (the European Parliament). There is also a federal administration (the European Commission which prepares policy proposals and guards the constitution). However, though, as in the US via Congress, it is the EU Council of Ministers, together with the EP, which legislates, there is no directly elected equivalent of the US President as head of government, who can also veto legislation. It is also true that the individual 50 states which comprise the USA have considerable legal autonomy. There is also, as this report has been examining an independent central bank.

However, notwithstanding these structural similarities, the key difference remains that the individual EU member states have, *voluntarily*, formed an evolving alliance with shared sovereignty. Moreover, individual member states are able, as the UK is currently demonstrating, to leave, without this being termed secession. This situation also means that any progress towards greater shared sovereignty must also be voluntarily entered into and confirmed in constitutional terms. Hence, though it is possible to amend the US constitution, and via the US supreme court to 're-interpret' the constitution, both paths to change are not easily managed, particularly the former.

The challenges presented to the EU, *in terms of its evolution,* are thus considerable and it is not clear that the US experience offers much assistance, despite the structural similarities indicated above. Rather does the European experience of Germany and Switzerland provide better models. In Switzerland the experience was over a 42-year period of moving from a confederation of 21 independent cantons in 1815 to the formation of the Swiss Federation in 1847 (with a further strengthening of federal power in 1874). In Germany, the experience was over a longer period from 1815, with a confederation of 39 sovereign states to 1871 with the formation of the German empire, excluding Austria, and dominated by the Prussian states.[1]

The German model may appear initially to be a useful way forward for the EU. The second chamber, the Bundesrat, which represents the Länder (regional states) is made up of delegates from the Länder governments, with larger Länder having more representatives, giving a form of weighted voting (as in the EU Council of Ministers). Indeed, the Länder forming the Bundesrat have power to challenge and even veto the federal authority.

In the Swiss model, partly related to the historical tradition of direct democracy, the representatives in the second chamber are directly elected from the cantons, are independent of the canton governments, and have the power to initiate legislation. (This has similarities to the US constitutional position). It is also the case that individual cantons may enact different social, economic, and political policies.

Given the evolution of the EU from a core economic alliance between states – and in this report we have been concentrating on monetary policy and the role of the ECB, and economic policy more widely – the more prescriptive, executive cum cooperative German model offers a way forward with federal economic governance and an enhanced role for the European Parliament to provide democratic accountability. However, the sociological diversity across and within the member states of the EU is suggestive of a path via greater European communal identity and citizenship to enable a gradual transfer of democratic credibility to European institutions and their policy-making.

This is not to suggest that either the German or the Swiss model, no more than the US model, should be used as a blueprint for a potential evolutionary path for the EU to move from confederation to federation. However, the slow process of the progression since the 1950s – not made easier because of enlargement – may not necessarily suggest, on historical grounds, that it will not happen. In a globalising world they may be other forces which propel a more rapid evolution towards a federal EU.

7.2 The Need for EZ Reforms

The main drivers to move closer to a *democratic* federal architecture are economic rather than political. Hitherto, following the Monnet functionalist approach, this has been possible, with, albeit grudgingly, political consensus following on the economic integration agenda. As argued above, a *technocratic* creation of an eventual federal EZ, with democratic acceptance following on, appears more problematic than hitherto in the EU of 28 countries (soon to be 27, assuming the UK leaves). Whether a sufficient political will, across the EZ let alone the EU, can be found to permit a significant move towards the necessary federal democratic structures is currently an open question, as we have indicated in the previous section.

Nonetheless, the future economic development of the EZ is dependent on providing an answer to the need for greater democratic governance and legitimacy. Notwithstanding the survival of the EZ over the past turbulent period, following the impacts of the GFC, it is clear that change will be required if the next global financial and economic crisis, in whatever form it takes, is to be able to be managed by the EZ. The role of the ECB has been important in overseeing an inter-bank payments settlement system (TARGET 2, see Annex, below); in acting as a lender of last resort (though this terminology is rejected by German politicians) to provide essential liquidity to a number of EZ country central banks, and in pursuing a substantial monetary policy stimulus to assist in lifting the EZ out of recession.

Whether the austerity policies, effectively imposed on a number of southern EZ countries via the Euro-Group northern EZ countries led by Germany, were either necessary or sufficient to promote an economic recovery is doubtful. The 'loose' monetary policy of the ECB partly alleviated the problem of the absence of fiscal stimuli in the southern EZ countries, not assisted by similar policies in the stronger economies of the northern countries. The gradual EZ economic recovery may be as much due to the easing of the fiscal discipline in both southern and northern countries and the ability of economies gradually to recover, even in the absence of policy actions. It may certainly be argued that the harsh discipline to achieve more flexible labour markets in the periphery countries over a short period via austerity and deflation imposed by the Euro-group could have been better and more fairly achieved over a longer period with active fiscal policies in these countries, including higher investment. The loss of economic growth and high youth unemployment during this period of enforced change was not a price that need have been paid to suit an ordo-liberal agenda.

The Greek debt crisis and the other debt problems affecting Ireland, Portugal, and Spain point to not just the absence of a democratic fiscal authority, but the specific problem of not having a debt management/issuance system. Of course, if there was a proper EZ fiscal governance structure, i.e. a Treasury and an agreement to issue Eurobonds, perhaps via the ECB in the first instance, then the issue of heterogeneous debt positions among the Eurozone countries would be resolved. Given the implacable political opposition of Germany to this suggested solution it appears unlikely to be agreed any time soon. In the next section we consider the potential for EZ reforms and the wider implications for future EZ development.

Finally, and crucially, is the need to build in to any new construction the ability to devise and implement appropriate fiscal policies aimed at the appropriate management of aggregate demand across the participating EZ countries.

First we will consider the recently announced European Commission proposals for reform of EMU.

7.3 European Commission Proposed Reforms

The reforms proposed cover a number of areas. Some of these are proposals which may lead to subsequent Communications. Others are Communications which are for immediate consideration by the Council of Ministers and the European Parliament (and the other EU institutions such as the Economic and Social Committee).[2]

A proposal to establish a **European Monetary Fund** (EMF), anchored within the EU's legal framework and built on the well-established structure of the European Stability Mechanism (ESM). In recent years, the ESM has played a decisive role in safeguarding the stability of the euro area by assisting Member States to regain or maintain access to sovereign bond markets.

The EMF would build on the ESM architecture, with its current financial and institutional structures essentially preserved, including when it comes to the role played by national parliaments. It would thus continue to assist euro area Member States in financial distress. In addition, the EMF would provide the common backstop to the Single Resolution Fund and act as a last resort lender in order to facilitate the orderly resolution of distressed banks. More rapid decision-making in cases of urgency and more direct involvement in the management of financial assistance programmes are also foreseen. Over time, the EMF could also develop new financial instruments, for instance to support a possible stabilisation function. The European Parliament and the Council are invited to adopt this proposal by mid-2019.

A proposal to **integrate the substance of the (international treaty between the EZ states) Treaty on Stability, Coordination and Governance into the Union legal framework, taking into account the appropriate flexibility built into the Stability and Growth Pact** and identified by the Commission since January 2015. In 2012, the 25 signatory Member States legally committed to incorporate the substance of that Treaty into Union law five years after its entry into force, which corresponds to 1 January 2018. The European Parliament has also called for this. The proposal incorporates into Union law the main elements of the Treaty in order to support sound fiscal frameworks at national level and is fully in line with existing rules defined in primary and secondary legislation. The European

Parliament and the Council are invited to adopt this proposal by mid-2019.

A Communication on **new budgetary instruments for a stable euro area within the Union framework** setting out a vision of how certain budgetary functions essential for the euro area and the EU as a whole can be developed within the framework of the EU's public finances of today and tomorrow.

The Communication discusses four specific functions: a) support to Member States for structural reforms through a **reform delivery tool** and **technical support** at the request of Member States; b) a **dedicated convergence facility for Member States on their way to joining the euro**; c) a **backstop for the Banking Union**, through the EMF/ESM, to be agreed by mid-2018 and made operational by 2019; and d) a **stabilisation function** in order to protect investments in the event of large asymmetric shocks.

The Commission will present the necessary initiatives in May 2018 in the context of its proposals for the **post-2020 Multiannual Financial Framework**. (The EU works on a 7 year MFF, so post 2020 there will be new 7-year MFF.) The European Parliament and the Council will then be invited to adopt these proposals by mid-2019. For the period 2018-2020, the Commission is also proposing to **strengthen the Structural Reform Support Programme**, by doubling the funding available for technical support activities, thus reaching €300 million up to 2020.

The Commission is also proposing to test the new reform delivery tool in a pilot phase. To that end, it proposes **targeted changes to the Common Provisions Regulation** governing the European Structural and Investment Funds (ESIF) in order to extend the possibilities to use part of their performance reserve in support of agreed reforms.

The European Parliament and the Council are invited to adopt these latter two proposals in 2018.

A Communication spelling out the possible functions of a **European Minister of Economy and Finance** who could serve as Vice-President of the Commission and chair the Eurogroup, as is possible under the current EU Treaties. By bringing together existing responsibilities and available expertise, this new position would strengthen the coherence, efficiency, transparency and democratic accountability of economic policy-making for the EU and the euro area, in full respect of national competences. Reaching a common understanding on the role of the Minister by mid-2019 would allow setting it up as part of the formation of the next Commission. The Eurogroup could then also decide to elect the Minister as its President for two consecutive terms in order to align both mandates.

7.4 Assessment of Commission Proposals

The Commission's proposals, set out above as a 'programme' of reforms, three of which are the subject of specific Communications, are ambitious. Less so in terms of their substantive content than in the number and comprehensive nature of the changes and in respect of the tight timescale proposed for their agreement. Of course, the Commission does not expect either the totality of the proposals to be agreed or that the suggested timescale will be met.

There are a number of proposals with which we can agree, but also some of the proposals appear to perpetuate a constricted approach to the need for a more flexible economic policy approach for the EZ and to ignore the requirements for strong democratic decision-making and oversight to be introduced.

We will leave aside the areas of agreement between our proposals and the Commission's – notably the proposal for an EMF and on the Communication of creating a European Minister of Economy and Finance – and concentrate on the concerns we have on some aspects of the Commission's proposals. However, as we indicate later, the establishment of an EMF on a substantial basis going beyond the Commission's tentative suggestion and implying the development of a federal budget, rather than simply an adjustment fund to assist in rectifying balance of trade deficits.

Though the Commission proposals are welcome, an initial reading suggests that on the two key issues of resolution of the balance of payments equilibrium within the EZ and the provision of sufficient freedom of fiscal action for individual EZ countries the proposals are heavily constrained in practice. It is clear that the Commission recognises these two key problems and the need to have active fiscal policies at central and national levels, as well as a central monetary policy via the ECB, but is unwilling to bring forward sufficiently radical specific policies. The problem, to be fair, is that the lack of willingness of some EZ countries, e.g. Germany, and some EU countries, e.g. Hungary and Poland, for different reasons, to adopt a more federalist approach. Germany is reluctant to move beyond a confederal EZ/EU, while governments in Hungary and Poland are endorsing an ethnic nationalism which appears unlikely to support moves towards federalism.

Other Suggestions

Before going on to discuss our own proposals it is worth describing the two proposals made in a *Levy Institute* paper, May 2016.[3] We believe that both are economically feasible and worthy of merit. However, we do not believe that they will be politically acceptable, at this point in time. Nonetheless, they should be put on the table for future consideration.

The first, is a proposal for using the Target 2 balances to effect the restoration of balance of payments equilibrium within the EZ.

'A more modest, yet more realistic, proposal would be simply to introduce symmetric and increasing charges on positive and negative Target2 balances. A similar measure would induce surplus countries to play their part in restoring balance of payments equilibria by adopting expansionary policies (such as tax cuts or wage increases) in an effort to encourage imports. Moreover, the proceeds of the charges could be used to finance investments, possibly through the European Investment Bank or European Investment Fund. The possibility of introducing such charges should fall entirely under the current capacities of the ECB, without representing a form of fiscal transfer between member states and without infringing on other EU regulations.'

The second, is a proposal to introduce a 'fiscal currency', similar to the WIR (*Wirtschaftsring-Genossenschaft* – Economic Circle) parallel currency in Switzerland and used since 1934. (N.B. The unit of account of the WIR-franc (CHW) is the Swiss Franc (CHF): one WIR-franc always equals the value of one Swiss-franc. But according to the WIR Bank's statutes, WIR-Credit cannot be redeemed for Swiss Francs.[4] This design criterion guarantees that money remains within the cooperative circle. In WIR, no 'physical' currency is printed or minted. WIR-credit is purely electronic. Since 1995, it is possible to make payments using a single plastic charge card rather than using cheques. In 2008 internet-banking became available.)

The aim would be to use the fiscal currencies (say *fceuro*) – which would *not* be convertible to euro or be legal tender – but could be used by governments to fund public expenditure (and to an extent, substitute for tax payments). The fiscal stimulus to domestic demand would be constrained so as not to either increase the trade deficit nor to compromise the fiscal balance targets agreed with the EZ authorities.

Though such a system would work, effectively by providing a fiscal mechanism to permit a fiscal expansion, albeit partly constrained by staying within externally set trade deficit or fiscal balance targets, without threatening the credibility of national bond issues. However, it seems unlikely to find favour politically and we have not endorsed the mechanism as viable politically at this point in time. Nonetheless, it is a suggestion which the European Commission should examine with a view to producing a Communication.

7.5 Our Prescriptions for EZ Reform

Economic Issues

Despite the problems with the Monnet functionalist approach there are some technocratic changes which might be made to the EZ structure and functioning.

Rather than try to persuade the Germans to accept direct fiscal transfers (which they will currently not agree) the argument should be focused on the notion of an EZ fund (the EMF) in the form of a federal budget. Given the bad political blood spilt in the wake of GFC and the consequent loss of European solidarity, the idea of fiscal transfers from one country to another is itself a source of political controversy. The argument should be focused on the need for an EZ fund (EMF) in the form of a federal budget. This should be presented as a reformed ESM to deal with *trade imbalances*, within the EZ. This will not be easy, but there is already agreement that one-third of any adjustment of EZ trade imbalances should be placed on the surplus countries.

This suggestion, though modest, will nonetheless be likely to encounter German, and other EZ/EU country, objections. The small federal budget (ESM/EMF) could be based on equal contributions, rather than proportionate ones. This would *partly* counter the immediate German reaction that they are paying for others inability to generate export and budget surpluses.

(It should be recognised that in a modern monetary economy, all other things being equal, trade surpluses will generate budget surpluses; via the Godley accounting balance identity,[5] i.e. with both *initially* public and private sectors in balance, a country with a trade deficit will import capital thus leading to a *matching* public sector deficit. Conversely, a country with a trade surplus will export capital leading to a *matching* public sector surplus). The contributions would be equal but the disbursements would favour the trade deficit countries, while the economic adjustment was taking place.

Additionally, and noting the fiscal currencies device discussed briefly above, there is a need to abandon the harsh austerity policies imposed on the EZ periphery countries. These policies have been *successful to the extent* that these countries have significantly reduced imports and marginally increased exports to move towards current trade account balances. However, the deeper and longer-lasting negative impact on unemployment and lost economic growth has been the price paid for the 'stabilisation' of the overall EZ economy. (The output losses or growth foregone, calculated as a percentage of GDP, is markedly different for core and periphery EZ countries. The mean average for core countries, 2008-2011 was 21%, in contrast to the 56% for periphery countries.[6] The cut-off date for this database is 2011. A recent update by the European Systemic Risk Board points out that sovereign debt crises, a feature of the periphery, greatly exacerbates output loss.[7])

There is no political or economic reason for symmetric fiscal policies to be applied to all EZ countries, particularly when part of the problem – excluding the element relating to the GFC – is because of asymmetric trading policies by some countries. This part of the problem needs to be dealt with directly. By expanding domestic demand in the surplus currencies; preferably voluntarily (noting above the suggestion of taxing TARGET 2 surpluses.

This issue of the asymmetry between the export-led northern European countries and the consumer-demand led southern European countries also impacts on the differing views on completing the Banking Union, in relation to the current *impasse* on agreeing the European Deposit Resolution Scheme (EDIS).

Political Issues

In the case of the EZ, the political situation, even in principle, is unsatisfactory. While ostensibly operating within a legal remit, provided by the TFEU, the operational technicalities are unable to be satisfactorily covered in this manner. On monetary policy it is correct that the Council of EZ Banks is nominally the supreme authority, in practice it is the ECB Board which takes the monetary policy decisions. On fiscal policy it is the undemocratic and dysfunctional Eurogroup of EZ finance ministers, supported by a secretariat, which takes decisions. In effect, this is inter-governmentalism masquerading as federalism, based on an intergovernmental protocol of the Lisbon treaty.

Moreover, the situation is patently less democratic than in the US. There is no formal, democratically mandated EZ government. This lacuna is incapable of being bridged without fundamental reform of the EZ architecture.

In the context of moving to a confederal structure, with federal elements, it is clear that new governance arrangements are required within the Eurozone, and indeed more widely in the EU as a whole.

There are three main barriers to any reform of the current unsatisfactory EZ situation.

First, German opposition to any move towards a more federalised governance structure is strong and represents a powerful block to any progress. The formal position of Germany towards the EU itself, as expressed in the position of its constitutional court, is that the EU is to be regarded as, and to remain as, a *confederal* entity. Coupled with this constitutional legal position is a clear fiscal economic view that any move towards an autonomous EZ fiscal authority which may deviate from the ordo-liberal, social market principles which underpin Germany's economic behaviour is likely to be opposed. This does not rule out changes in the governance arrangements of the EZ, but these would have to be confederal rather than federal in nature.

Second, from the inception of the 'European project' in the 1950s constitutional progress in the EU has been via the 'Monnet functionalist' approach. Essentially, this entails making technocratic changes in advance of public opinion and waiting for that opinion to confirm the new position. Indeed the construction of the current dysfunctional and undemocratic EZ is an example of the functionalist approach; hence no move, initially, to a full-blown federal structure. However, the shift to an anti-elitist, part-populist political environment across Europe (and the US) almost certainly consigns the functionalist approach, if not in its entirety, to history. Hence, any changes – and we wait to see whether the initiative started by President Macron will find sympathy with the new German Coalition government – are likely to be slow and incremental and will need to have at least majority EZ/EU public opinion behind them, before their enactment. Third, and linked to the above two considerations, is the potential need for EU treaty change. Given the problems with agreeing the Lisbon Treaty there is no appetite for further changes. It may be possible to avoid full treaty change via an international treaty between the EZ countries. However, though this might be way forward it is neither ideal nor would it be without its own difficulties in terms of securing agreement among the current 19 countries or a short amendment to the Lisbon Treaty, as before (2012).

Lest this iteration of barriers to a significant move forward from the current confederalism towards federalism appears pessimistic, it is not meant to be. What is required to be able to move forward is a realistic appraisal of the difficulties in the way of change. It also suggests that the European Parliament may be the key to unlocking the gateway to achieving, albeit slowly, a clearer perception among the peoples of the EU of the necessity of change. Change which will both protect them from the social damage associated with the global financial crisis and deliver the steady social development and economic growth which characterized the early decades of the EU.

7.6 EZ Changes

Any such international treaty, if required, would need to cover a number of issues. These would include, as indicated below, an enhanced role for the European Parliament in terms of scrutiny and democratic accountability. Hence, whatever the possible outcomes as far as EU-wide treaty change are concerned there must be a number of specific changes in the way in which the EZ is governed and economic decisions are made, without democratic oversight.

A further change which could be made, though it is not clear whether it would require treaty change, would be to transfer the formulation of fiscal policy papers from the Eurogroup Secretariat to the European Commission. This would place the EZ in the same position as the EU in terms of policy proposals. The final decision would remain in the hands of the Eurogroup, with added consultation with the EP, preferably prior, but certainly after any policy decision had been taken.

The appointment of a EZ Finance Minister (EZ-FM), separately from the Eurogroup of finance ministers, has been suggested by a number of organisations, including now the *European Commission*, and also by President Macron of France. We now offer our own suggestions for the role, powers, mode of appointment, and democratic accountability for such an office. Such a reform would not require treaty change, but is the ultimate direction in which other lesser reforms should be moving. The European Commission proposal is very close to our own proposal summarised below, including an enhanced role for the European Parliament.

Role: An EU-FM would act as a political authority safeguarding the economic and fiscal interests of *the Eurozone as a whole*, as opposed to the interests of individual member states.

Powers: The main powers of the EZ-FM would be to (i) oversee the coordination of EZ fiscal and economic policies, (ii) enforce rules in case of non-compliance, (iii) coordinate spending investment decisions by EU/EZ funding mechanisms across the EZ to be approved by the EZ Eurogroup by qualified majority voting, (iv) ensure compatibility between fiscal policies pursued by the EZ and the wider EU. The EZ-FM would be responsible for the management of the European Monetary Fund, an improved version of the European Stability Mechanism.

Mode of appointment: The EZ-FM post would be member of the European Commission and President of the Eurogroup. However, the appointment would be made directly by the EZ Heads of State, subject, as with the ECB President, to scrutiny by the European Parliament. This procedure would facilitate coordination of fiscal and economic policies between the EZ and the wider EU. The term of appointment would be 5 years. If it was necessary to dismiss the person appointed, for whatever reason, this decision would be made by the EZ Heads of State, in conjunction with the European Parliament.

Democratic accountability: The EZ-FM would chair all meetings of the Eurogroup and would be responsible for reporting on the fiscal and economic policy decisions made to the European Parliament. This would also provide democratic scrutiny at EU level of decisions made by the Eurogroup, in relation to the use of investment funds and the EMF.

7.7 The Role of the European Parliament

Following the establishment of the ECB, the European Parliament was to receive regular annual reports from the ECB and the President of the ECB appears regularly before the relevant Committee of the Parliament.

Since the entry into force of the Lisbon Treaty in 2009, the European Parliament has participated as equal co-legislator in the ordinary legislative procedure in establishing detailed rules for multilateral surveillance (Article 121(6) TFEU). This involves, inter alia, the preventive part of the Stability and Growth Pact, as well as more diligent macro-economic surveillance to prevent harmful imbalances following the financial crisis. The 'six-pack' (see 3.5 above) strengthened Parliament's role in the economic governance of the EU, in particular through the introduction of the 'European Semester' and the installation of an 'Economic Dialogue'. In addition, Parliament is consulted on the following issues:

- agreements on exchange rates between the euro and non-EU currencies;
- the choice of countries eligible to join the single currency in 1999 and subsequently;
- the appointment of the President, Vice-President and other members of the ECB Executive Board;
- legislation implementing the excessive deficit procedure provided for in the Stability and Growth Pact.

By contrast, the EP role in relation to the Eurogroup is not defined and is lacking in being able to have even cursory transparency and accountability. At a minimum, the EP role in relation to the fiscal policy operated by the Eurogroup should be equivalent to that exercised in relation to the ECB and its conduct of monetary policy.

On the assumption that there are no fundamental changes to the structure of the EZ, this should entail:

- the appointment of the President of the Eurogroup, who should appear regularly before the relevant Committee of the EP
- the appointment of the Secretary of the Eurogroup Secretariat
- consultation on the fiscal policy of the Eurogroup, following receipt of the minutes of the meetings of the Eurogroup

Were there to be the appointment of a Finance Minister of the EZ, presumably replacing the current President of the Eurogroup, then this post would also be subject to the same accountability procedures as indicated above.

7.8 Some Reflections from a USA Viewpoint

The federalist objectives of the EU/EZ, though not shared by all EU member states, will have to be approached more along the lines of the Swiss Federation rather than the USA. Nonetheless there are a number of elements of the US constitution which might be applied, and a number which should perhaps be avoided.

In the case of the US, the Administration is, in principle, both easier to monitor and influence in republican democratic terms than is the case in the EZ, given the formal constitutional structures of the US, via the various Congressional Committees.

The US federal government preceded the formation of the US central bank. In *formal* democratic terms, and in practical operation terms, the political influence which may be exerted over the Federal Reserve is considerable, in contrast to the current position in the EZ. Even in the US, the democratic control over central bank decision-making tends to be *post facto* and hence indirect, with time-lags involved. It is unlikely that any improved democratic accountability within the EZ as far as *monetary policy*, via the ECB, is concerned will go beyond the formal position in the US, but this should be the objective.

In relation to the *fiscal policy* in the US there is the ability to exert influence on the *political* decisions involved in promulgating fiscal policy. The aim in the EZ should be to similarly influence the fiscal policy decision-making, currently in the, insufficiently undemocratic, hands of the Eurogroup.

More generally, though it is tempting to look at the US federal system as a model for the EZ/EU, and in some areas this may be instructive, care should be taken to note the very different historical, functional, cultural, and democratic evolution of the two political geographical areas.

Indeed, if one wanted a model for the evolution of states from confederal structures and functioning to more federal structures then either the development of the Swiss Federation, or Germany itself, would be more appropriate political models.

As we suggested at the start of this chapter, the evolution of the EU into a group of federalised states will not be an easy or a rapid matter. In some ways it may be able to learn from the experience of the USA, but the construction off a federal EU will have be tackled essentially *sui generis*. Moreover, its evolution will be influenced by external global factors as much as by internal discussion and constitutional reform.

Notes

1. Clive H. Church and Paolo Dardanelli, 'The Dynamics of Confederalism and Federalism: Comparing Switzerland and the EU', *Regional and Federal Studies* 15.2 (2005), pp. 163-185.

2. The relevant Communications are as follows:
   Communication on further steps towards completing the Economic and Monetary Union – COM(2017) 821
   Proposal for the establishment of a European Monetary Fund anchored in the Union legal framework – COM(2017) 827
   Proposal to integrate the substance of the Treaty on Stability, Coordination and Governance into the Union legal framework – COM(2017) 824
   Communication on new budgetary instruments for a stable euro area within the Union framework – COM(2017) 822
   Targeted changes in the Common Provisions Regulation to mobilise funds in support of national reforms – COM(2017) 826
   Proposal to strengthen the Structural Reform Support Programme – COM(2017) 825
   Communication on a European Minister of Economy and Finance – COM(2017) 823.

3. M. Amato, L. Fantacci. D. Papadimitriou, G. Zezza, 'Going Forward from B to A? Proposals for the Eurozone Crisis', *Levy Economics Institute*, Working Paper 866. <http://www.levyinstitute.org/publications/going-forward-from-b-to-a-proposals-for-the-eurozone-crisis>

4. Richard Douthwaite, *The Ecology of Money* (Green Books, 1999), Ch. 2.

5. Wynne Godley, Marc Lavoie, 'Fiscal policy in a stock-flow consistent (SFC) model', *Journal of Post Keynesian Economics*, 30.1 (2007), pp. 79-100.

6. 'Systemic Banking Crises Database: An Update' IMF Paper prepared by Luc Laeven and Fabian Valencia, WP/12/163, pp. 24-26.

7. 'A New Database for Financial Crises in European Countries', Occasional Paper Number 13, July 2017, European Systemic Risk Board, pp. 23-24. The mean average for the periphery is taken from output losses for Greece, Ireland, Portugal, Spain and Italy; the core from Austria, Belgium, France, Germany,

Federal Central Banks

Luxembourg and the Netherlands. Finland did not qualify in the database as a systemic crisis.

Chapter 8
Conclusions and the Way Forward

What then may we conclude from this examination of the issues relating the centralised role and operations of central banks in the context of federal governance structures? And what 'forward guidance' might we be able to offer both the EU and the US in this regard?

1. There is an inevitable tension between the technocratic imperatives of central bankers and the need for democratic control through the federal political process and structures. To an extent this is resolved through the 'concordat' which provides operational control by the central bank while the wider political economic parameters are set in the political system.

2. In the US, this is established, constitutionally, via the

Federal Reserve Board receiving its mandate and being accountable to Congress. What this means in practice is less clear in these days of rapid technocratic decision-making by the Federal Reserve, with only *post facto* accountability to Congress. Given that this type of rapid technocratic decision-making has come to characterize modern economies and modern monetary systems, it may be argued that it is important to avoid an over-centralization of *monetary policy* decision-making power in the hands of central banks. However, given the inter-relations between wider fiscal and other federal policy interventions and decisions across the federation in spatial terms, in practice this is, as we have illustrated problematic.

3. In the EU, or more particularly the Eurozone (EZ), the increasing concentration of monetary policy is perhaps more clearly seen. Unlike in the US, the ECB is the only supra-national/federal institution within the EZ. Unless there is a concerted attempt to surround the ECB with a governance structure – not simply rely on the broad constitutional legal limitations – then there is a danger that either too much technocratic power will be exercised by the ECB. This *executive technocratic* federalism is also exhibited in relation to the current economic governance structures of the Eurozone (EZ), currently in the hands of the undemocratically accountable EZ Eurogroup and its secretariat.

4. There is an urgent need to establish an accountable fiscal authority at EZ level, in the form of an EZ Finance Minister. However, this position needs to be at the head of a Treasury function with a federalized budget. This will be a reversion to the earlier postulated European Monetary Fund. This fund would have two dimensions. The first may be seen as equivalent to the IMF in terms of providing support to EZ countries having balance of

trade and payments problems. The second may be seen as representing the beginnings of a federal budget, perhaps linked to a EZ-wide unemployment insurance scheme. In this latter connection the already existing ability to utilise European Investment Bank financing would mean two automatic counter-cyclical elements in the EZ federal budget structure.

5. In this manner the over-centralised nature of EZ economic policy, relying on monetary policy which is necessarily set centrally would be gradually overcome. The Member States of the EZ would still be able to pursue their own separate budgetary and other economic policies, in the context of a federal budget able to act contra-cyclically as necessary and, via the European Parliament (EP) exert influence of overall federal economic policy. In this context the EP would fulfill a similar role to that of Congress in the US.

6. In time it might also be the case that the current independent central banks in the EZ countries would become, as are the regional federal reserve banks in the US, become branches of the ECB. In this manner an evolution of the EZ towards the Federal Reserve model in the US might be accomplished.

7. However, this is not an agenda for the short-term confederalist evolution of the EZ/EU. Rather should the initial policy concentration be on the further development of the Banking Union. With the two of the three EBU pillars (the Single Supervisory Mechanism and the Single Resolution Mechanism) agreed there is an urgent need that some form of European Deposit Insurance System (EDIS) is agreed – perhaps in an incremental manner – to ensure an adequate coverage of risks at EZ level, with adequate funding. In this context, and more generally, it will be necessary for a reduction in the asymmetry between

the export-led Northern European countries and the consumer-demand led Southern European countries to be reduced, but not entirely at the expense of the Southern European countries.

8. Both in the case of an evolving EZ and in the US, the theoretical basis on which the two central banks operate, and their democratic legitimacy and accountability require attention. There is a clear danger that the return to basing central bank policy on the discredited 'loanable funds' approach, in which interest rates are seen to be equilibrating savings and investment, will lead to an overweening belief in the efficacy of monetary policy. In the case of the US and more particularly the EZ/EU, there is a necessity for a more balanced approach between monetary and fiscal policy, and a combined approach to managing aggregate demand, via an, albeit limited, federal budget as far as the EZ is concerned.

9. Examining the formal role, actual operations, and accountability in a federal democratic setting demonstrates the lacunae in considering the aspects of central bank operation. It seems clear that there are unaccounted for regional social and economic impacts involved with an over-reliance on a centralized monetary policy. Hence, though there is a defined need for a centralized payments settlement system covering the commercial bank system, with the provision of a lender of last resort function, the operation of monetary policy, working in tandem with fiscal policy, is a matter for federal democratic control and accountability.

10. But though a central bank is a key federal economic institution in both the existing US federation and in the developing confederal EZ/EU, it needs to be seen as *one* institution, situated in a constitutionally legitimized and democratically administered structure. Moreover,

those federal/confederal structures should be continually analysed, revised, and refreshed, particularly in the context of a globalising financial world. The global financial crisis demonstrated a number of design flaws, both in the US and, particularly because of its 'immature' status as a federation, the EZ/EU. The next decades need to see reform and development to ensure a greater resilience than demonstrated in the 2008 to 2010 period and thereafter.

Annexe

The Target System: A Brief Description

The TARGET 2 (Trans-European Automated Real-time Gross Settlement Express Transfer System) is essentially a system for settling accounts, in real time, between banks within the Eurozone, and is owned by the Eurosystem of Eurozone banks. It reflects the cross-border transactions of the 19 Eurozone countries.

All modern central banks have real time gross settlement systems (RTGS) which enables the national central bank to provide reserves on demand when required by individual commercial banks which run short of liquidity to settle accounts with other commercial banks. This is obviously true of the Federal Reserve in the USA.

Hence, the objectives of TARGET 2 are:
- to support the implementation of the Eurosystem's monetary policy and the functioning and stability of the euro money market
- to minimise systemic risk in the intra-Eurozone payments market
- to increase the efficiency of cross-border payments made in euro.

TARGET 2 Started in 2007 and from 2011 all 19 Eurozone countries had migrated on to the system.

The availability and cost of liquidity are two crucial issues for the smooth processing of payments in RTGS systems. In TARGET 2, liquidity can be managed very flexibly and is available at low cost since fully remunerated minimum reserves – which credit institutions are required to hold with their central bank – can be used in full for settlement purposes during the day. The averaging provisions applied to minimum reserves allow banks to be flexible in their end-of-day liquidity management. The overnight lending and deposit facilities also allow for continuous liquidity management decisions.

The Eurosystem provides intraday credit. This credit must be fully collateralised and no interest is charged. However, all Eurosystem credit must be fully collateralised, i.e. secured by other assets. The range of eligible collateral is very wide. Assets eligible for monetary policy purposes are also eligible for intraday credit.

Under Eurosystem rules, credit can only be granted by the national central bank of the Member State where the participant is established.

Banks' treasury managers have a keen interest in the use of automated processes for the optimisation of payment and liquidity management. They need tools that will allow them to track activity across accounts and, where possible, make accurate intraday and overnight funding decisions from a single location – e.g. their head office. TARGET 2 users have, via the Information and Control Module, access to comprehensive online information and easy-to-use liquidity management features that meet their business needs.

The Target System: Some Controversy

Despite the unexceptional nature of TARGET 2 it became the subject of discussion, and controversy, when in 2011 Professor Sinn of the Ifo in Munich produced a study suggesting that the sheer size of the TARGET 2 balances, and particularly the net *creditor* balance of Germany at 326 billion euro at the end of 2010, matched by corresponding *debtor* balances by the Southern European countries who were running trade deficits.

Sinn's Views

Sinn argued that the increase in Target liabilities is a direct measure of net payment orders across borders, i.e. of the portion of the current account deficit that is not counter-balanced by capital imports, or, equivalently, the sum of the current account deficit and net capital exports. Indirectly, they also measure a country's amount of central bank money created and lent out beyond what is needed for domestic circulation.

Since every country needs a relatively steady amount of central bank money for its domestic transactions, payment orders to other countries, which reduce the domestic stock of money, must be offset by a continuous issuing of new refinancing credit, i.e. the creation of new central bank money.

Similarly, the increase in money balances in the country whose central bank honours the payment orders reduces the demand for fresh refinancing credit. Hence, a country's Target liabilities also indicate the extent to which its central bank has replaced the capital markets to finance its current account deficit, as well as any possible capital flight, by creating new central bank money through corresponding refinancing credit. Sinn illustrated that, from an economic perspective, Target credit and formal rescue facilities serve the same purpose and involve similar liability risks. Sinn's presentation on 19 May 2011 at the Munich Economic Summit motivated an op-ed column in the Financial Times. They reconstructed the data on the basis of the balance sheets of the Eurosystem's national central banks and the balance-sheet statistics of the International Monetary Fund.

Later, in June 2011, Sinn and Timo Wollmershaeuser compiled the first panel database of the Eurozone's Target balances. The authors point out that the additional creation of money by the central banks of the crisis-stricken countries was provided by a lowering of the standards for the collateral that commercial banks have to provide to their national central banks to obtain refinancing credit. Furthermore, they showed that the commercial banks of the Eurozone's core countries used the incoming liquidity to reduce the refinancing credit they drew from their national central bank, even lending the surplus liquidity to this central bank, which implies that the Target balances indirectly also measure the reallocation of refinancing credit among the countries of the Eurozone. The authors showed that the national central banks of the northern countries became net debtors to their own banking systems. Sinn and Wollmershaeuser argue that the euro crisis is a balance-of-payments crisis, which in its substance is similar to the Bretton Woods crisis. Moreover, they purport to show the extent to which Target credit financed current account deficits or capital flight in Greece, Ireland, Portugal, Spain and Italy. They also show that the current account deficits of Greece and Portugal were financed for years by refinancing credits of their national central banks and the concomitant Target credit. They document as well the Irish capital flight and the capital flight from Spain and Italy, which began in earnest in summer 2011.

The two authors compare the Target balances of the Euro-system with the corresponding balances in the *US settlement system (Interdistrict Settlement Account)* and point out that US ISA balances relative to US GDP have decreased thanks to a regularly performed settlement procedure in which ownership shares in a common Fed clearing portfolio are reallocated among the various District Feds comprising the US Federal Reserve System. They advocate the establishment of a similar system in Europe to end the ECB's role as a provider of international public credit that undercuts private market conditions.

The problem is that Sinn's arguments are misconceived. A number of authors, e.g. Lubik and Rhodes (2012), *Federal Reserve Bank of Richmond* have criticised Sinn's approach. Lubik and Rhodes, for instance, argue, correctly, that

'TARGET2 does not *cause* those problems. It merely *reflects* the long-term lending and collateral policies of the ECB and the relative strength of national economies within the Eurosystem. Placing arbitrary limits on TARGET2 balances at this stage would not solve anything. To the contrary, TARGET2 restrictions would unnecessarily constrain cross-border transactions and ultimately defeat the purpose of the EMU'. (My italics)

There are, of course, differences between the Federal Reserve System and the Eurosystem. *In the USA* all the Reserve Banks are owned by the federal government. Hence as all Federal Reserve banks are owned by the federal government, a loss in, say, Richmond is irrelevant as there is an equivalent gain in New York. *In the Eurozone*, however, the ECB is effectively owned by the national governments, via their national central banks (the Eurosystem), and not by the European Union *per se*. The TARGET 2 system is decentralised in a way in which the Federal Reserve system is not. The gains and losses will appear as liabilities and assets in the TARGET 2 system.

Hence the liabilities expressed within the TARGET 2 system are not 'debts' as Sinn suggests, but merely accounting representations of the cross-country capital movements within the Eurozone. It is important, therefore, not to confuse the impacts of monetary policy decisions, *including the provision of liquidity based on acceptable collateral*, taken by the ECB with the process of payment and settlement of central bank money, and intra-group payment flows, as part of the normal business of the Eurosystem of banks under TARGET 2. In respect of liquidity TARGET 2 minimises the need for the available liquidity, it does not itself create extra liquidity.

The problems about which Sinn is concerned are inherent in the non-federal nature of the Eurozone and the 'insecure' nature of the Euro. Within the federal USA monetary system there is a virtual zero chance of the dollar being supplemented by an alternative currency. The same cannot be said for the confederal nature of the Eurozone monetary system. The discussions about Greece leaving the Eurozone and even the possibility of Italy also, indicate the relative fragile nature of the Euro. But the changes to the TARGET 2 system would seriously weaken not only the TARGET system but also the Eurozone.

Of course the hidden agenda of Sinn is to shift to a Northern European Eurozone, so his proposals are not surprising.

Concluding Remarks on TARGET 2

TARGET 2 should be viewed as a necessary and effective mechanism to manage the cross-border movement of bank money, resulting from cross-border payments deriving from trade and capital transactions, within the ambit of the ECB. The settlement system parallels the system used by Western central banks, including the Federal Reserve. At a time of turbulence, such as that relating over a number of years to the impact of the global financial crisis (GFC), the trade and capital flight imbalances which accompanied the GFC were *reflected* in the debit and credits attributed to the national central banks which form the Eurosystem; but were not (and are not) *caused* by them. They are no debts created. There is, of course, one key difference between the Federal Reserve System and the Eurosystem in that the US system operates within a fully federal, whereas the Eurosystem operates within a confederal system.

Italy: A Postscript

While taking this Report to publication stage, the Italian elections were held in March 2018 leading to an uncertain outcome. The pro-European Union centrist parties were greatly reduced, replaced by the break-away and Euro-sceptic Northern League and the popular protest party, Five Star Movement. Difficult coalition talks lie ahead and despite some of the anti-EU rhetoric of the campaign it is most unlikely that the Italian situation will resemble the UK's decision to leave the EU. That said, the European Council will have at its table a major economy, and founder EU and EZ country, whose government will oppose the current direction of reform by the EMU and ECB (as discussed in our Report).

Italy goes almost unmentioned in our Report. Like many European economies it was hit hard by the GFC and the subsequent recession in its economy. It was spared the humiliation of conditional bailouts from the ESF and it was the unconditional promise by the ECB President, Mario Draghi, to do whatever it takes that stopped the rapidly climbing interest rates for Italian bonds. Italy has every reason to be grateful to the ECB, in finally acting –indirectly– as the lender of last resort. Equally, Italy is both a polity and economy that is unwilling to adapt to the strict demands of the EMU and ECB, and the underlying assumption that all EZ societies are ready and able to conform to standard model and are as plastic as warm putty.

Whatever final government outcome of the 2018 election, it should not be regarded as an *existential* threat to the Eurozone. Italy does have unresolved banking problems, but as in other European states there are practical solutions able to resolve its non-performing loans. The politics of this process within EZ institutions will be of a different order from the process already described in our Report. The politics is containable without crisis, and below we first outline a way of proceeding. But the negotiations could well crystallize the tensions between the dominant economic model of the northern bloc member states and its unsuitability for many southern European states. We assess this at the end of the Postscript and ask whether these issues now have to be treated as other than, and more than, regional or periphery problems.

Politics

As always with Italian politics, caution should be observed before reaching for the panic button. Neither of the parties who were the main victors in the elections – the Northern League and the Five Star Movement – campaign on leaving the Eurozone or the EU. Nor have equity markets taken fright, though the yields on bonds has fallen.

What exactly will be the make-up of the next government is not yet clear, but it is possible that discussions between the two largest parties could result in a coalition government. One aspect of the result is that, effectively, the Northern league covers the north of the country and the Five Star Movement covers the south of Italy. This division between north and south has been a perennial political problem for many decades.

There is a likelihood that the new Italian polity will resist any severe attempt by the EZ to force the country either to cut its high debt to GDP ratio or to introduce further austerity measures. Around 58% of Italians approve of the Euro, but it is a large country and one of the founding members of the EU and it seems unlikely that the EZ would attempt to 'bully' Italy in the way it did to Greece.

The Italian Economy

As far as the Italian economy overall is concerned the recovery noted in 2017 is expected to continue with GDP growth of 1.5 % in 2018; a current account surplus maintained; inflation at a low level, but with fears of deflation subsiding; investment is also increasing, and unemployment remaining high, but not increasing, and employment growing. The various tax reforms and small-scale bond investment reforms introduced by the previous government appear to be having a positive impact.

The public sector deficit is within the 3% Fiscal Compact limit, though the debt to GDP ratio, at around 130% is well beyond the target 60% ratio. Nonetheless the vast majority of this debt is owned by Italians themselves, including small investors; similar to the position in Japan where the debt ratio is 70% higher. On the other hand private debt to GDP has been falling since 2014 and is the lowest in the Eurozone, aside from Germany.

The Italian corporate sector – 30% of Italian GDP is in manufacturing – has been assisted by the ECB's corporate bond buying programme, currently due to stop in September 2018. ENEL (electricity and telecoms) and ENI (oil and gas) have been major beneficiaries, as have major Italian banks. As the economy is growing there appears not to be any major concern about the future of ENEL or ENI. The Italian banking sector, particularly the two major banks Unicredit and Intessa Sanpaulo (Italy's small banks are mostly savings and cooperative banks) which have most of the Non-Performing Loans (NPLs).

Italian Bank Holdings of Non-Performing Loans (NPLs)

As far as the banking sector is concerned the measures introduced, essentially forced mergers, of the Banco di Sienna and the two Venetian banks have resolved the immediate problems of the banking sector. Moreover, via the *Atlante* programme over 100 billion euro of NPLs have been sold to the private sector, with some guarantees from the state. However, there are there are still 300 billion as of June 2017 of non-performing loans on the books of Italian banks; around a third of all Eurozone non-performing loans. (N.B. *It is worth pointing out that some of the NPLs are more precarious than others. One problem is that in a number of cases the 7-year legal process for bringing cases to court means that some busi-*

nesses will not make loan payments until the last minute even though they are able to do so). This position obviously poses risks and is concerning EU and national regulators and the market. However, following ECB guidance on the management of NPLs, there is some reduction in NPLs from 2016 to 2017 (pws Italia Report, December 2017).

Under the Bank Recovery and Resolution Directive (BRRD) the problem should preferably be resolved by a bail-in, as in the case of Cyprus. In Cyprus the main bearers of costs were Russian oligarchs holding large sums in Cypriot banks. Even so the bail-in was contentious, despite the logic behind the action.

The problem in Italy is that this bail-in solution will impose costs on millions of Italian bond-holders/taxpayers across the board. Given the improving economic perfor-mance of the economy and the higher levels of equity held by EZ banks, including Italian banks it is not clear whether holding on to the loans poses a major risk, either to Italy or to the EZ. But the concerns remain and EZ/ECB atti-tudes have hardened; more strongly favouring bail-ins over bail-outs, e.g. the BRRD. The delay in Italy addressing the problem – in comparison with Spain which dealt with their NPL problem in 2012 by a mixture of bail-out and other bail-in and bank merger measures – means that the country is facing a tougher political climate at EZ level.

In any event, an alternative to a bail-in, i.e. a partial bail-out is still possible and would make sense. A mixed solution would be:

- to allow the banks to hold a third of the NPLs on their books, for sale for a strictly time-limited 2 years
- a further third of the NPLs were the subject of purchase by the Italian government on behalf of the taxpayer (which could subsequently achieve profitable return

- a final third of the NPLs should be the subject of a bail-in

Such a mixed solution would be beneficial to both Italy *and* the EZ. It simply requires flexibility on the part of the EZ. Not to relax the current 'moralistic economic' and inflexible approach would be to repeat the mistakes made in relation to the earlier Greek crisis, but with far more severe repercussions in the case of Italy.

Conclusion

Ultimately, for the EZ, the Italian banking problem is an issue of how to manage risk. As the Governor of the Italian Central Bank, Ignazio Visco, also an ECB Governing Council Member, has recently said 'Diminished trust among member states has led to a sterile conflict between calls for risk reduction versus those for risk sharing. These proposals are instead complementary.' (*Assiom-Forex conference in Verona, March 17, 2018*). To whomsoever, he was referring, the statement is correct.

The NPL problem besetting Italian banks, including crucially five of the larger banks is resolvable, providing flexibility. To adopt an unreasoning 'hard line' in terms of enforcing bail-in for the whole of the NPLs, risks damaging the economic recovery of Italy within the Eurozone and throwing the EZ into an entirely unnecessary crisis.

www.ingramcontent.com/pod-product-compliance
Lightning Source LLC
Chambersburg PA
CBHW072132270326
41931CB00010B/1740